WHO REALLY DECIDES
WHAT NEWS YOU SEE, HEAR AND READ?

Whether your main source of information is a student
newspaper or the evening news on national TV, media
decision-makers select and control what you know—for
better or for worse. This unique book takes you inside
this crucial decision-making process. It shows you reporters, editors, broadcasters, advertisers and government
officials in action, and it invites you to match your judgment against theirs. It provides realistic, practical insight
into such issues as "censorship," "bias," and "the public
interest"—plus new tools for evaluating and improving
your entire information environment.

POWER TO PERSUADE

"A provocative and eye-opening book . . . pointing out
with concrete documentation just how easily a story or
an insight can be slanted either by word selection or by
emphasis."

—Publishers Weekly

D1042994

ABOUT THE AUTHOR

ROBERT CIRINO was born in San Fernando, California. Prior to teaching in secondary schools, he worked as a truck driver and merchant seaman. In 1962 he received a B.A. degree in social sciences from San Fernando Valley State College. He did further work at San Diego State, and received a Master of Secondary Education degree from the University of Hawaii in 1968. His first book was *Don't Blame the People* (1971), a study of bias in the mass media. His articles have appeared in *Television Quarterly*, *The Review of Southern California Journalism*, and *Grassroots Editor*. He currently lives in Honolulu.

POWER TO PERSUADE: MASS MEDIA AND THE NEWS

Robert Cirino

BANTAM PATHFINDER EDITIONS
TORONTO / NEW YORK / LONDON

RLI: VLM 12 (VLR 9–12+)
IL 11–adult

POWER TO PERSUADE: MASS MEDIA AND THE NEWS
A Bantam Book | March 1974
2nd printing ...... May 1975   3rd printing .... August 1976

ISBN 0-553-10182-X

Published simultaneously in the United States and Canada

Bantam Books are published by Bantam Books, Inc. Its trade-
mark, consisting of the words "Bantam Books" and the por-
trayal of a bantam, is registered in the United States Patent
Office and in other countries. Marca Registrada. Bantam
Books, Inc., 666 Fifth Avenue, New York, New York 10019.

PRINTED IN THE UNITED STATES OF AMERICA

Contents

A popular Government, without popular information, or the means of acquiring it, is but a Prologue to a Farce or a Tragedy; or, perhaps both.

—James Madison
Fourth President of
the United States, 1832

The issue before us ought to be stated starkly. It is, quite simply, who is to retain the potential to rule America. We know, if we are honest with ourselves, which segments of the economic and social structure have the loudest voices in the decision-making process in Washington. But the *potential* for popular check remains. It remains, however, only so long as the people can obtain education and information, only so long as they can communicate with each other, only so long as they can retain potential control over the mass media of this country. So long as we preserve the people's *potential* to rule—their *potential* opportunity to participate in the operation of their mass media—there is some hope, however small, that some future generation—perhaps the next—will use this potential to rebuild America.

Nicholas Johnson
Federal Communications Commissioner
In testimony to the Senate
Subcommittee on Communications, 1969

Acknowledgments

I am indebted to the students at Fulda Junior High School and Huntington Park High School. Without their frankness, integrity, and criticism I would not have been motivated to write this book. Thanks to the many dedicated journalists, professors, and critics who have written books and articles analyzing the mass media. I have noted their contributions in the footnotes and bibliographies. This book would have been impossible without the use of the UCLA, University of Hawaii, Los Angeles, and Redondo Beach public libraries. Many thanks to my brother, Don Cirino, and to Alma Aki and Kathy Sohl for reading the manuscript and making suggestions for improvement. I am also grateful to Toni Burbank at Bantam Books for her editorial suggestions.

Robert Cirino

Preface

This book is based on the belief that the vast majority of human beings, if exposed to competing ideas from an early age, will make better decisions than a dictator or an elite group elected by a public that is not exposed to all viewpoints. People thus informed will more likely decide on reasonable, practical, just, and humanitarian policies because in the long run it is in their interest and their country's interest to do so. Democracy is based on the faith that man's best thinking will emerge if he is given a choice from among ideas that compete fairly in the public marketplace.

Today's public marketplace is the mass media—our television, radio, daily newspapers, and mass-circulation magazines. And, in that marketplace, we are all consumers of the information products the mass media put forth.

The purpose of this book is to help the citizen develop a better understanding of the production, control, and dissemination of informaion by the mass media. This understanding will enable him to detect and compensate for one-sided propaganda, to make better choices among information sources, and thus to participate more effectively on both an intellectual and practical level in the democratic process. Through increased participation a citizen can experience more satisfaction and self-awareness than if he or she either withdraws from society or passively absorbs the persuasive messages produced by the mass media. Since our society ultimately depends on the people, through their periodic voting, to make major policies, an increased level of citizen participation and awareness will also help our society to better meet its present and future challenges.

The method of this book is to provide actual case studies in the production, control, and dissemination of mass media products. Each case invites you to retrace the decision-making process just as if you were a media executive, editor, or reporter. You will be faced with the day-to-day problems of creating a fair marketplace of ideas. Whether or not you agree with the final decisions made, each case should help you become a more aware information consumer.

Surveying Your Information Environment

In the United States, all representative viewpoints—from the radical left to the far right—have freedom to publish. But, since the publications of some viewpoints are unpopular, attract little advertising, or are poorly distributed, not all citizens are exposed to them.

In order to find out whether you are being exposed to a competitive marketplace of ideas, you need first to be aware of what information products you are consuming.

HOW TO MAKE YOUR OWN READING CHART

On the following chart, list every publication that you read regularly, classifying it in two ways. First, decide what kind of a publication it is. Is it national or local? Does it deal primarily in news and public affairs or in other topics of general or special interest? Second, decide how liberal or conservative each publication is by asking what, in your opinion, seems to be the overall bias, message, or orientation—radical, very liberal, liberal, conservative, very conservative, or far right?

At this point, it doesn't matter whether anyone else agrees with your classifications or whether you can justify them fully. If you are not sure what the overall viewpoint is, make an approximate choice anyway. You are merely surveying the opinions you *now have* about the publications you are presently reading. Use your own idea of what a radical, liberal, conservative, or far-right viewpoint is—not somebody else's.

After entering the name of the publication in the proper spaces of the column, add a permanent mark opposite it to indicate the magnitude of what its perspective reads in the leading? This grids to the march. Of to give to the points fifth answers to as magnetic to might to these

What I Read

Publications Read Regularly	The Spectrum of Political Viewpoints						
	Radical	Very Liberal	Liberal	Conservative	Very Conservative	Far Right
National weekly or monthly news and public-affairs magazines						
Local weekly school, college, "underground," or community newspaper						
Daily newspapers						
Other publications of general or special interest (on literature, fashion and homemaking, humor, history, science, sports, personal relations, hobbies, etc.)						

2

After entering the name of the publication in one of the columns, add in parentheses the approximate number of minutes per week that you spend reading it.

This chart is not meant to be a test of any kind. The only thing you should be concerned about is how accurately it reveals to you your current reading habits and information consumption.

HOW TO MAKE YOUR BROADCAST CONSUMPTION CHART

Most Americans spend much more time watching television and listening to the radio than they do reading. The average household has the television on seven hours a day, and the average adult listens to his radio (at home, at work, or in the car) four hours a day. Today, 64 percent of Americans of voting age depend on television as their major source of news and, by a wide margin, they find it more believable than newspapers, magazines, or radio.

Using the following chart, figure out how much time, on the average, you spend watching TV or listening to the radio. If you watch one movie or football game a week, divide the time of that one program by seven to get the daily average.

You may have some difficulty trying to determine the political viewpoint of some types of programs. In classifying entertainment or music, ask yourself what the overall message was and how it made you feel about society or politics. For instance, the pregame or half-time ceremony at a football game may make you feel that America is great the way it is and should be left alone. You might classify it as "moderate to conservative." On the other hand, a folk song program may make you feel that the American system has some faults and that radical change is needed. You might want to call this "liberal to radical."

Remember, there is no right or wrong judgment about the range of political bias that you find ex-

Broadcast Consumption

Type of program	Average amount of time per day (in minutes)	Range of political viewpoints expressed
Local TV news programs		
Local TV public-affairs programs (documentaries, interviews, or specials)		
Network TV news programs		
Network TV public affairs programs		
Local or network TV entertainment programs		
Local or network TV sports programs		
Total TV time per day _____		
Local or network radio news		
Local or network public affairs		
Local or network radio entertainment (including music)		
Local or network radio sports		
Total radio time per day_____		

pressed in certain types of programs. This is merely a survey of your own opinions.

Looking at the two surveys, you can see that your information consumption falls into certain patterns. If you wish, make out charts for your parents, brothers and sisters, or classmates, so that you can compare your patterns with theirs.

You can now decide whether you are receiving all of your information from just one or two viewpoints, or whether you are being equally exposed to the entire spectrum—from the radical left to the far right. Have you made up or are you making up your mind about important issues without having heard or read what every representative viewpoint has to say?

If you answer yes to this last question there are probably two reasons why. First, people naturally tend to read or listen to ideas that reinforce what they already believe or want to believe. Second, the extremes on the political spectrum do not have as much communications power as the moderate viewpoints. In order to get some points of view, you would have to go to the library or subscribe to a special weekly newspaper or magazine. Since many people do not have enough time, money, or reading ability to do this, they depend on the cheapest, most easily consumed, and most powerful information agencies—television, radio, daily newspapers, and mass-circulation magazines. Most of these agencies tend to be moderate in their political orientation.

COMMUNITY INFORMATION SURVEY

Who has communications power in your community? To find out, form a small group to investigate the major information sources in your area.

1. Who owns the daily newspaper or newspapers, local weekly newspapers, radio stations, and television stations? Are the stations affiliated with any network or

are they independent? Does the newspaper subscribe to any nationally syndicated features? (A syndicated article is one that is used by many newspapers the same day.) Most of this information can be obtained by asking the stations or newspapers themselves.

After you find out who owns the mass media agencies in your community, try to find out if the owners own other businesses. For example, does the newspaper owner also own a radio or television station, a paper mill, or a book-publishing house?

You will probably discover some interesting patterns of ownership. Many recent observers have noted a nationwide trend toward monopoly in the mass media. Fewer and fewer companies are owning more and more newspapers and stations. As reported in the December 1972, *Columbia Journalism Review,* only 4 percent of American cities had competing daily newspapers in 1972. More than 60 percent of daily newspaper circulation is held by chain publishers (publishers who own more than one newspaper). One-fourth of the total revenue of daily newspapers (approximately $2.2 billion) is earned by the ten largest chains.

Those who own both print and broadcast agencies (cross-media owners) control 36 percent of daily newspapers, 25 percent of TV stations, 8.6 percent of AM radio, and 9.5 percent of FM radio. Chains, cross-media owners, conglomerates, and firms related to mass media control a total of 58 percent of daily newspapers, 77 percent of TV stations, 27 percent of AM radio, and 29 percent of FM radio.

The eleven largest cable TV companies have half of all cable television subscribers. Broadcasters and newspapers own 37 percent of cable television.

2. Although it is not part of the mass media, another important element of the information environment—especially for a student—is the libraries. How many are there in the community? Which daily newspapers, local weekly newspapers, and national news and public-affairs magazines do they subscribe to? Make

a spectrum chart for the library's newspapers and magazines like the one you made for yourself. In your opinion, or in your group's opinion, does the library offer publications from the entire spectrum of viewpoints? Are you taking advantage of the diversity that the library does offer?

3. In the future, Community Antenna Television (CATV)—usually referred to as cable television—will become an important part of your information environment. Cable TV has the potential of offering a clearer picture, two-way communication (enabling the viewer to participate in a program or shop for groceries via his TV), reception of stations from other towns, and as many as eighty-four channels.

You or your group should investigate the present situation regarding cable television in your community. Find out if the franchise to operate cable has already been granted to a cable company by your city council. What does the franchise agreement say? Who owns the company? How many other businesses or cable systems does the company own? How many channels does the system offer? Are there any channels set aside for citizens to use ("public-access channels")? How much does it cost to subscribe? How many and what percent of households subscribe?

If the franchise has not yet been granted, which cable companies are competing for it? Who owns them? What kind of cable service are they offering?

COMMUNITY TASTE SURVEY

The final factor to survey is your own media likes and dislikes. Answer the following questionnaires for yourself, and then go on to collect answers from your parents, classmates, neighbors, and other members of the community.

Television and Radio Questionnaire

1. On the average, how many hours per day do you spend watching television? listening to the radio?
2. What are your three favorite programs?
3. Are you satisfied with the variety and quality of entertainment programs?
4. Is there too much violence in entertainment programs?
5. Should the amount of violence in entertainment programs be restricted?
6. What news program do you like best?
7. What newscaster do you like best?
8. What commentator or editorializer do you like best?
9. Would you like to see more public-affairs programs during prime time television (7:30 P.M. to 11:00 P.M.) and early morning or late afternoon radio time?
10. Do you think newscasts and public-affairs programs, together, represent fairly all viewpoints on the political spectrum?
11. Does the total programming provide enough information to enable viewers or listeners to make intelligent decisions on major issues?
12. Do you think the overall effect of advertising on viewers is good or bad?
13. How often do you watch or listen to "public" or "educational" television or radio as opposed to commercial stations?
14. Should public noncommercial television and radio programming be decreased, kept the same, or increased?
15. Are you satisfied with the quality of children's programs?

Newspaper Questionnaire

1. How many days a week do you read the daily newspaper?
2. Which section do you like best (news, sports, comics, personal interest, family, etc.)?
3. Which section do you read first?
4. Is there too much or too little coverage of trivia (stories or pictures about animals, pretty girls, unusual but unimportant happenings, etc.)?
5. Is the newspaper providing enough information to enable readers to make intelligent decisions on local issues? national issues? international issues?
6. Do you think the newspaper fairly presents information and opinions from the entire spectrum of possible viewpoints?
7. Would you like to have two or three competing newspapers in town instead of just one?
8. Which source of news do you trust the most: television, radio, the daily newspaper, or a news magazine?
9. Which of the above sources do you think is the most biased?

Going over your own, your neighbors', and your classmates' answers to the questionnaires, do you find that you are basically satisfied with the information and entertainment you are getting? Do you think that citizens in your community are being adequately exposed to the kind of information that will enable them to make the best choices on important issues? Is it possible to like television, radio, and newspapers because they are entertaining, but at the same time feel that they do not present enough information or diversity to best serve the public need and interest?

Now that you are more aware of your community's information environment and your own habits of consumption, you will be asked to participate in and think about the actual production and dissemination of information in the mass media.

Introduction to the Cases

The test case at the beginning of each of the following chapters concerns an event that actually took place and demanded a decision by a media executive, producer, editor, or reporter. The decision greatly affected the production, management or dissemination of vital information. The possibility that these decisions may have kept you or your parents ignorant of important events, or of information that might have altered your opinions, should not be treated lightly.

Put yourself in the position of the person with the power and responsibility to make the decision. Imagine that your primary obligation is to provide exposure to all important information and viewpoints. But remember that you also have obligations to the news company you are working for. Your decision will not be easy for there are often conflicts between the two obligations.

There are no answers with which to judge whether you are right or wrong. Your decisions are merely expressions of your conscious or unconscious, consistent or inconsistent ideas about the role of mass media in a democracy. The answers the media executives made are not necessarily the right ones or, for that matter, any better than yours. By the time you finish this book, you should be able to evaluate your responses to the test cases and to explain why—in some cases—the decision was a hard one to make. You may even decide that a good decision was impossible given some circumstances and pressures.

Each chapter includes examples of cases similar to the initial test case, plus activities and questions designed to clarify the issues involved.

The chapters are followed by an analysis of mass media products and the issue of bias from the viewpoint of a consumer. Following these chapters, you will be given the chance to create a communications system that eliminates or counterbalances the shortcomings of our present system. The book concludes by suggesting what you can do to improve the communications system in your own community.

I

IS OBJECTIVITY POSSIBLE?

When a reporter decides what story to cover, which facts to look for, whom to interview, how to begin and end the story, and which words to use, can he avoid making choices that reveal his personal attitude? Can he write the story in such a way that no person, organization, or viewpoint is made to look any better or worse than the facts or truth merit? Will the reporter's vision be the same as that of other reporters?

When an editor who receives the reporter's story decides whether or not to use it, what part to cut, the words for the headline, the space and placement allotted to it, the accompanying photograph, and the sentence for a caption, can he avoid making choices that reveal his own attitudes? Will his choices be the same as those made by other editors handling the same story?

When a newscaster reports a story, will his tone of voice, emphases, pitch, facial expressions, and posture indicate his own attitudes toward the story? Will they be the same as those another newscaster uses?

These are difficult questions for journalists: those who believe they can be objective will answer yes to each. They are convinced their personal attitudes do not influence their professional decisions, and that their products are without bias of any kind. This has been the official credo and guideline for professional journalists for many decades.

Other journalists don't believe they can be totally objective, but they do believe they should strive for objectivity. They are convinced that this striving produces the best possible news products, even if they are not without some degree of bias.

A third group of journalists, the so-called new journalists, depart sharply from their colleagues. They not only believe objectivity is impossible for a human being, they believe that journalists should not even strive or pretend to be objective, since this restricts their writing and deceives the public. They feel that the decision to adopt an objective style is in itself a biased decision and that it tends to support established authority. Instead of striving for objectivity, they strive to discover and reveal the truth as they see it without trying to hide their personal attitudes. Some of them think reporting should be a tool for bringing about desirable change in society. They are called "advocacy journalists." Like their fellow "objective" journalists, however, they still subscribe to other traditional journalistic standards such as fairness, correct attribution and quotation, accuracy, and reliability.

In the next seven chapters you can try your hand at reporting, editing, and newscasting. You should gain a better idea of whether objectivity is possible and which kind of journalism best serves the public.

1

Choosing Words

TEST CASE

The year: any time from 1963 to 1973. You are the new managing editor of a newspaper and are establishing a policy of word usage.

Will you use the word "allies" or the word "mercenaries" in referring to Asians (Meo tribesmen and Thai troops) who are being paid to fight on the side of the United States in Southeast Asia?

Will you ever use the words "propaganda" or "indoctrination" to describe news coming from either U.S. daily newspapers and stations or from the U.S. government even though you know that at times it is biased, misleading, or even false?

Compare your decision with the one that mass media actually made in this situation.

Except for very liberal and radical publications, no news agencies in the United States routinely referred to Asian troops paid by the U.S. as "mercenaries."

Most U.S. daily newspapers and stations seldom use "propaganda" or "indoctrination" to describe news products coming from the mass media or from government information sources. These words are usually reserved for describing the news coming from countries that have government-controlled communications systems or that are hostile to the United States.[1] As Bernard Kalb of CBS reported one evening, China "turned its big propaganda guns on President Nixon." [2]

Certain words are powerful tools for depicting the mood of an event and for discrediting or ennobling people, organizations, and causes. Such words may be chosen intentionally, unconsciously, or even by chance. But the words still have a bias and can affect the news consumer's attitude whether he is aware of them or not.

Robert O'Hara, author of *Media for the Millions,* has described how words can also be used to create stereotypes:

It is the choice of just the right adjective or verb to sum up a situation that evokes from the receiver the response the communicator feels should be adopted toward a story. . . . The word and the situation it describes become almost inseparable, so that the use of the word triggers a standardized response in the receiver. . . .

They use stock words and phrases to describe the same situations, which give the news an appearance of sameness. The event being described is news, but it is described in terms applied over the years to similar events. The impression of sameness obscures understanding and limits the range of possible responses for the receiver.[3]

Those who are aware of this power of words can communicate better themselves and detect more easily the misuse of words in the mass media.

MEDIA DECISIONS

1. In describing men, the media usually use words that refer to occupational position and talents ("expert craftsman," "brilliant lawyer"). But in describing women, these same media usually ignore occupation, talent, or accomplishment by using words that refer to marital status or physical attributes ("grandmother," "housewife," "mother," "divorcée," "blonde," "pert,"

"vivacious," "curvaceous"). When boys turn eighteen years of age they are referred to as adult "men," but women from eighteen to eighty are often called "girls." Further, the media reinforce the pro-male bias in our language by continuing to use male terms for positions of importance ("congressman," "chairman," "spokesman") even when those positions are held by women.

2. Prior to 1936, none of the mass media would use the word "syphilis." In 1934, Dr. Thomas Parron, New York health commissioner, was scheduled to talk about the disease on a network radio station's program called "Public Health Needs." He sent an advance copy of his statement to the station; it included the word "syphilis." He was told by a network executive: "We can not mention the word syphilis on the air." When Dr. Parron refused to delete the word, the station canceled his appearance and announced it could not begin the program due to "circumstances beyond our control." [4] In place of Dr. Parron, they put on a piano player.

The Associated Press wire service refused to use the word until 1938 when the same Dr. Parron, in his first news conference as surgeon general of the United States, forced the wire services to do so by warning that he wouldn't hold another news conference without repeatedly using the dreaded word. The general manager of the AP then decided to use it, but ordered it to be put in quotes to indicate that it didn't originate from the AP.

Even after 1938, in a classic case, one network allowed the dramatization of a program on syphilis to be shown, but only on the condition that the disease not be mentioned by name.[5]

3. To describe President Truman, a Democrat, while he was in office, *Time* magazine typically used such phrases in news reporting as "said curtly—said coldly—flushed with anger—the petulant, irascible president—publicly put his foot in his mouth—with a blunt finger he probed."

To describe Republican President Eisenhower in their news reports, *Time* wrote: "said with a happy grin—cautiously pointed out—said warmly—devastatingly effective—serene state of mind—frankness was the rule—brisking aside misunderstanding." [6]

The use of biased words in news magazines was not unusual in the Eisenhower period. The University of Syracuse School of Journalism undertook the task of searching for word bias in the news coverage of the 1956 political campaign. The survey found that *Time*'s words were 75 percent biased to favor the Republicans and *Newsweek*'s 28 percent to favor the Republicans. [7]

4. In selecting words to describe their actions or policies, organization and government public-information spokesmen often choose words that conceal the truth or minimize the brutality of certain actions or policies. In reporting the war in Vietnam, the Defense Department news releases contained many such words. In general, the mass media channeled these words to the public without questioning their use until the later stages of the war.

The following are a few of these "official" words (in the left column) compared to more explicit, concrete, or factual words (on the right):

"nontoxic resources control"	chemical defoliation or crop destruction
"limited air interdiction"	heavy bombing in Laos or Cambodia
"area denial"	use of antipersonnel devices
"search and destroy"	destroy and then search
"relocation"	forced transfer of civilians
"incursion"	invasion
"elements in the credibility gap" / "evidence of lack of candor"	lies

5. In a study of network newscast bias during the 1968 presidential campaign, Edith Efron found that

euphemistic words were often used to the advantage of those who used violence for political ends:

Violent mob outbreaks are called "restlessness"; violent disruptions of people's rights of free speech are called "protest"; violent assaults on persons are called "heckling"; violent provocations of the police are called "confrontations" or "demonstrations"; violent assaults on property are called "liberating buildings"; thefts of property are called "commandeering"; acts of arson are described as "fire dances"; radicals shrieking abuse at candidates and threatening to destroy society are called "youth." [8]

ACTIVITIES

1. Go through one page of both your school and daily newspaper (or tape a local newscast) and make a list of all the adjectives, verbs, and adverbs that contain a judgment in their description of a person, group, or activity. Note whether the implied judgment is negative or positive.

2. Select any article in your school or daily paper's sports or news sections that seems to have a lot of value-loaded adjectives, adverbs, and verbs. For each positive word use a negative word, and for each negative word use a positive word. How does this change your feeling about the event or person described?

3. Write a short news article covering a friend's behavior during a class period or lunchtime. Use only the facts as you saw or discovered them, but use words that make him look admirable.

Write the story again, using words that make him look foolish or despicable.

QUESTIONS FOR DISCUSSION

1. Should a news agency use the name a group or nation gives itself, or a name given by a hostile govern-

ment? For example, should China be called "Red China" or the "People's Republic of China"? Should a news agency have a policy of using the names all groups and nations have chosen for themselves, or should the agency give this privilege just to groups it approves of?

2. In describing people, groups, events, or countries, is it possible to use adjectives, adverbs, and verbs that are completely objective or neutral?

3. Is it possible to describe a violent or warlike activity as if it was peaceful or a peaceful activity as if it was violent?

4. Is it possible that the public's judgment of a person or group is determined as much by the one-sided use of biased words over a long period of time as it is by the facts or events that constitute the content of the news?

How can citizens, news agencies, and politicians cope with the use of biased words?

2

Creating Headlines

TEST CASE

The year: 1972. You are the chief copy editor of a large newspaper. What headline would you give to the following story?

A government report, Television and Growing Up: The Impact of Television Violence, has established, for the first time, that there is a causal relationship between violence in television programming and violent behavior for a certain type of children who make up a small minority, but for the vast majority television violence was found not to cause violent behavior.

Compare your headline with the one that an editor actually wrote in this situation.

The New York Times headline read: *TV VIOLENCE HELD UNHARMFUL TO YOUTH.*

As an article in the Columbia Journalism Review pointed out, the headline could just as well have emphasized that "for the first time a causal connection between television violence and violent behavior had been established, if only for a minority." Two members of the commission that disclosed the findings criticized the Times headline as misleading. They said that the commission report reached no conclusion to justify a statement that television violence was unharmful to youth.[1]

Headlines are supposed to give an accurate summary of the story and at the same time to tempt the reader to read it. Reporters do not write headlines for their own stories. This is done by an editor, and only after the page number and the amount of space merited by the story have been decided. The editor must write a headline to fit the space allotted, and he must do it quickly. It is therefore easy to make a mistake that can mislead the reader. It is also easy to use intentionally biased words so that the reader adopts a desired attitude.

Since our impression of many events is formed by reading headlines alone—without reading the stories—the use of a biased word or phrase to summarize a story should be a matter of serious concern to the news consumer. Even if a headline is not obviously biased, the consumer might ask whether a different word, phrase, or emphasis would be just as accurate and whether it would leave the reader with a different impression.

MEDIA DECISIONS

1. David Brinkley, on the "Huntley-Brinkley" newscast, headlined a report on President Nixon's 1971 budget by stating that it proposed no drastic change in priorities. He went on to demonstrate this by showing a chart illustrating that the $73 billion proposed for defense was twenty-nine times more than the $2.5 billion budgeted for natural resources and pollution control.

The *Los Angeles Times*, reporting on the same story, used this headline: NEW BUDGET: MORE FOR LIFE THAN WAR; NIXON BEGINS REORDERING OF U.S. PRIORITIES.[2] It emphasized that the *total* amount proposed for health, education, and welfare was greater than the $73 billion proposed for defense.

2. In August 1966, Edwin Reischauer, former ambassador to Japan, gave a speech about the U.S. policy in Vietnam. In covering this speech the *New York Times* headline stated: REISCHAUER CRITICAL OF VIET POLICY.

The *Washington Post* coverage of the same speech was given this headline: REISCHAUER BACKS U.S. VIET POLICY.[3]

3. The *Chicago Tribune* published an article detailing the legal actions being taken by the women's liberation movement to end sexual discrimination. The article included an assertion by a women's liberation spokeswoman that no one in the movement had ever burned a bra.

The headline writer nevertheless gave the story this headline: WOMEN'S LIB: LAWSUITS REPLACE BRA BURNING.[4]

4. A CBS-radio affiliate reporter in Honolulu (KHVH) covered a campaign statement by Michigan Governor George Romney in which Romney stated that the Vietnam War was the number-one issue in the 1968 presidential campaign. The story was headlined: ROMNEY IS THE ONLY CANDIDATE TO PUT THE NEGRO IN SECOND PLACE.

The news item itself didn't mention Romney's stand on the racial issue or even the word "Negro."[5]

5. The text of a *Los Angeles Times* story evaluated the results of the 1968 Poor People's March on Washington and Resurrection City in this manner: "The government made some meaningful concessions. Undoubtedly, because of Resurrection City poverty has been brought to the American consciousness as never before."

The story was given this headline: BURIED IN MUD: FOUNDED ON HOPE, RESURRECTION CITY DIES IN IGNOMINY.[6]

ACTIVITIES

1. Using biased headlines on the sports page is a practice accepted by both journalists and readers. Try to rewrite the sports headlines of your daily paper substituting neutral or factual words for colorful or loaded expressions.

Look through the news section of the paper—where using biased headlines is not accepted—and list any headlines that use loaded words similar to those you found on the sports page. Rewrite these headlines using more neutral words.

2. Take the front page of your school or daily newspaper and cut out each article. Cut the headlines off and put them into an envelope. Read each story and make a headline of your own that best captures the essence of the story. Compare your headlines with the originals. Which is the better headline for each story? Is either obviously biased?

3. Choose four important front-page stories from your daily paper about national or international events. Go to the school or community library and find one or two daily newspapers from different cities and list the headlines they used for the same stories. For each story, briefly explain why you think one newspaper's headline was more informative and accurate than the other.

QUESTIONS FOR DISCUSSION

1. Is it possible for an editor to write a completely objective headline, or one that will be considered objective by all viewpoints? Why?

2. If a newspaper used headlines that were often unfair to a person, group, or country, but the reader wasn't aware of this headline bias, do you think it

would affect the way he or she feels and thinks? How much different would the news consumer think and feel if the bias was just the opposite for an equal length of time? What would be the result if the reader was exposed equally to both biases?

3. Which has the most impact on the greatest number of people: the headline or the story?

3

Creating Captions and Narrations

TEST CASE

The year: 1970. You are the president of a television network news department. Your own reporters and film crew have not been allowed into North Korea for some time, but you have purchased a recent film made there by Wilfred Burchett, a Communist journalist from Australia. You feel that the film is definitely worth showing to the American people as it covers many facets of life in a country they know little about. However, you feel Burchett's narration is biased to favor the Communist government in North Korea.

Will you eliminate his commentary and have one of your own reporters supply what you feel is a more objective narration? Or will you keep the original narration and comment on its bias either before or after the film is shown?

Compare your decision with the one that a network executive actually made in this situation.

CBS showed the Burchett film on morning and evening newscasts but had one of its own reporters, who was not on the scene when the film was made, supply the narration. His narration focused on the use of propaganda in North Korean government and society.[1]

Every news photograph has a caption; every segment of television news film is accompanied by dialogue or narration. People want to know who is in the picture, what they are doing, and when and where the event took place. Everyone needs some assistance in placing what they are seeing in a larger context. But, along with the necessary explanations, the news consumer may unknowingly be absorbing a bias carried—intentionally or not—by the words, phrases, or questions that are selected for the caption or narration. Without his being aware of it, the bias may affect the way the consumer judges the event or person portrayed in the photograph or film. He may not read the story underneath or hear anything that would cause him to question his impression.

In controlled testing with college students (each group of students was shown the same photograph, but with captions that had contrasting biases) it was found that students developed significantly different attitudes toward the persons in the photograph solely because of the bias in the caption.[2]

The alert consumer can help protect himself against biased captions and narrations by asking what other word, phrase, quotation, or emphasis would have been just as accurate or appropriate.

MEDIA DECISIONS

1. Men in the Irish Republican Army (IRA) consider themselves fighters for Irish independence from Britain. Many people opposed or unsympathetic to the IRA view these men as terrorists.

Under a 1971 photograph that showed an Irish Republican Army man holding a rifle and kneeling under an Irish tricolor flag, the *Irish Independent* newspaper had this caption: "An IRA man . . . above him hangs a tricolour." Under the same photograph, *Life* magazine had this caption: "A professional IRA terrorist . . . crouched beneath the Irish Republican tricolor." [3]

2. In 1968, NBC News purchased a film from a free-lance Czech cameraman that showed Russian trucks and tanks invading the Czechoslovakian city of Košice. Although the cameraman's notes claimed that the people were throwing rocks at the trucks, the half-hour film showed no rock throwing. The crowds were shown milling around, and there were only a few seconds of film depicting some broken windows on the trucks. Nevertheless, the news producer tried to create dramatic action by splicing together the few shots of broken windows with shots of the crowds moving about. The narration for the 2 minutes and 25 seconds of edited film was based mainly on the unconfirmed notes of the Czech cameraman, and it emphasized violent details that were not actually heard or shown in the film. As Chet Huntley narrated the report on NBC's evening news:

> The Czechoslovakians' rocks could not stop the Russian tanks, but they did smash the windows of many Soviet trucks. . . . Hundreds of people shouted insults at the invaders. Many hurled rocks and stones . . . and some broke up paving blocks to use against the invaders. [4]

3. In 1969, after a period of border clashes between the two countries, a Chinese and an Indian soldier posed for a photograph on the India-China border. The photograph showed the two soldiers pointing their guns at each other across a barbwire fence.

The *Washington Daily News* used the caption "Tense moment."

Under the same photograph a *Life* magazine caption read "Friendly hijinks." [5]

4. The 1968 CBS documentary "Hunger in America" included a filmed segment of a baby dying. The

narration explained that the baby had died of hunger. It was later revealed that the baby had in fact died of premature birth.[6]

5. The 1971 NBC documentary about conservation, "Say Goodby," ended with a dramatic scene of a polar bear apparently being shot dead, its cubs wandering aimlessly. The narration said: "Grieve for them. . . . Grieve for us."

Actually the polar bear wasn't killed; it was merely shot with a tranquilizer gun. Yet this fact was omitted from the narration, leaving the audience to believe unquestionably that the polar bear was shot dead.

ACTIVITIES

1. Go through your school or daily newspaper and cut out four photographs without their captions. Then read the story that accompanies each photograph and, without looking at the paper's caption, make up your own. Try to be informative, accurate, and neutral. Have a friend read the same stories and write captions. Compare your captions with his and with the newspaper's. How do you account for the differences?

2. Go through your school or daily newspaper (including sports and women's sections) and select three photographs with captions that express a judgment or opinion, no matter how slight or subtle. Read the stories that accompany these photographs and then write as neutral or objective a caption as you can.

For each of the same three photographs, write a caption depicting the subject as favorably as possible without being obviously biased.

Write a caption depicting each subject as unfavorably as possible without being obviously biased.

Of the three different captions for each photograph, which do you think most accurately reflects the truth the way *you* feel and see it?

3. Find a front-page AP or UPI photograph and story that deals with a controversial topic such as school busing, a Supreme Court decision, abortion, pollution, welfare, or defense spending. Then find one weekly newspaper published by the radical left (such as the *Guardian*) and one published by the far right (such as *Human Events*). Compare the captions under the same or similar photographs of the event. Can you tell from the captions alone how each of the three newspapers feels about the event or the issue? Which is the most biased caption? Which caption gets to the truth of the matter as you feel and see it?

4. Videotape the same news or sports story covered by different newscasts or sportscasts. Classify it as to political leaning, change the narration (instead of caption), and answer the questions as in the activity above.

QUESTIONS FOR DISCUSSION

1. How can the public judge for itself, after reading a story, whether the accompanying caption was misleading or a subtle expression of opinion instead of being merely a neutral description?

2. Assume that a photograph or film depicts the essence or truth of an event or person; for example, that a man is courageous, or that he is a liar. Should the caption notice or help bring out this truth even though it will imply a personal judgment by the caption writer? Or should the editor ignore what he or she knows to be the truth and select a neutral caption?

When you ignore what you know to be the truth about a person or event and instead produce a neutral caption, are you being objective or are you favoring the side that the truth would embarrass?

3. How many captions do you read without going on to read the entire story that accompanies the photograph? What has more power to influence the public's attitude—a caption under a photograph or a written paragraph in a story?

4

Deletion

TEST CASE

The year: 1970. You are the general manager of a large wire service. Your stories are used by thousands of newspapers and broadcasters both in the United States and around the world. You have just received a story from your Saigon office written by one of your most reliable and respected reporters who was on the scene in Cambodia. Part of his story reveals how some American troops were looting stores and houses. You feel that if this information were sent out over the wires it might cause violent or hostile responses from different groups and displease the U.S. government.

Will you omit that part of the story telling of the looting, or will you leave the story intact?

Compare your decision with the one that a wire service executive actually made in this situation.

Wes Gallagher, general manager of the Associated Press, deleted the part about the looting. As a result, the thousands of news agencies using the story passed on to their millions of readers a partly censored story. The AP foreign editor then wired the Saigon office to make it clear what they wanted from that office:

WE ARE IN THE MIDST OF A HIGHLY CHARGED SITUATION IN UNISTATES REGARDING SOUTHEAST ASIA AND MUST GUARD OUR COPY TO SEE THAT IT IS DOWN THE MIDDLE AND SUBDUES EMOTION. SPECIFICALLY TODAY WE TOOK LOOT-

*ING AND SIMILAR REFERENCES OUT OF ARNETT
COPY BECAUSE WE DON'T THINK IT'S ESPECIALLY
NEWS THAT SUCH THINGS TAKE PLACE IN WAR,
AND IN PRESENT CONTEXT THIS CAN BE INFLAM-
MATORY.*

*The cable went on to justify similar deletions in
another story and recommended: LET'S PLAY IT COOL.*[1]

Generally, news stories are supposed to be written
with the most important facts first and the least important last. This enables the editor who is short on
space to cut the story from the bottom up and yet not
lose any important facts. But sometimes, instead of
cutting from the bottom up, an editor will cut out
facts he thinks are irrelevant, in bad taste, or unveri-
fiable. Or he may cut out facts merely because he
doesn't want the public to know about them. He may
even cut out such information when there is no shortage of space or time for coverage. Whether the motive
is based on journalistic or political considerations, this
type of cut can give a story a considerable bias. Of
course, the news consumer has no way of knowing
what was left out; no blank spaces are left by the
editor to indicate a deletion. Such deletions might not
occur too often, but that doesn't minimize the effect
and importance of this type of editing. The deletion
of one or two sentences can significantly alter the
essence of a story. Furthermore, these same sentences
may contain facts that are so significant that exposure
to them just once may effect a change of attitude
toward an event or issue.

MEDIA DECISIONS

1. In a police raid on Chicago Black Panther headquarters in 1969, it was reported that a shoot-out had

occurred and that two Panthers, Fred Hampton and Mark Clark, were killed. Later, a grand jury found that the police had fired all but one of the nearly one hundred shots fired. As a result of this finding, the attorney general, Edward Hanrahan, and twelve policemen were indicted for concealing or altering evidence to make it appear that the Panthers had fired ten to fifteen times on the police as they entered the Panther apartment in search of illegal weapons. At the trial, startling new evidence was revealed by the prosecutor. He had uncovered transcripts of statements that four Panthers had made to their lawyers admitting that at least four shots had been fired by the Panthers. The same four had sworn before the grand jury that only one shot had been fired.

This new evidence played a key role in the dismissal of the case.

The *Baltimore Sun*, Chicago newspapers, and others took note of the new evidence in their story of the dismissal. But the *New York Times*, the *Washington Star-News*, and the *Atlanta Constitution* made no reference whatever to the new evidence in their stories of the dismissal.[2]

2. In late 1960, the "Huntley-Brinkley" newscast reported the following story:

> Financier Alexander Guterma was sentenced to eight to twenty-four months in prison today for acting illegally as an agent for Dominican dictator Trujillo.

Omitted from this item were the most important facts. Guterma wasn't just an ordinary Trujillo agent; he was a special kind of agent. While president of Mutual Broadcasting Corporation, he made an agreement with Trujillo whereby, in return for $750,000, his 450 affiliated stations would carry 425 minutes of news favorable to Trujillo "in the guise of genuine news" for a period of eighteen months.[3]

3. In 1972, the *Washington Post* and *Los Angeles Times* uncovered information disclosing that members of the Committee for the Reelection of President Nixon, including some who were closely linked to the White House and others who were former Central Intelligence Agency (CIA) employees, had used infiltration, eavesdropping, forgery, and acts of violence to try to sabotage and immobilize the Democratic party. The story was commonly referred to as the "Watergate affair."

CBS News, relying heavily on these newspaper accounts, produced a two-part report, the first of which was fourteen minutes long. After it was shown, a special counsel to President Nixon called a CBS executive on the telephone to talk about the report. After the call, the board chairman of CBS, William Paley, ordered the second part of the report cut from fifteen to seven minutes.[4] The head of CBS News later claimed that the cut was made to strengthen the story rather than to accommodate the White House.

4. A former producer of New York City's WPIX-TV "Clay Cole" show (a teen-age couples dancing program) testified at a Federal Communications Commission hearing that editing techniques were used to make it look as though there were fewer blacks in the audience than there actually were. He revealed that when this technique didn't work the station would delete live coverage and substitute earlier tapes that depicted the audience as predominantly white.[5]

5. In 1970, during the half time of a football game carried live on ABC, at the State University of New York at Buffalo, the band began performing its act called "Give Peace a Chance." It was critical of the war in Vietnam, racism, and pollution.

Roone Arledge, president of ABC Sports, blacked out the half-time performance of the band because, as he said, "It was an editorial to get out of Vietnam," and thus was political in nature. In place of the half-time show, ABC reviewed football scores for more than five minutes.

Later in the season ABC Sports carried live the half-time show of the Army-Navy game featuring the introduction of four soldiers who took part in the Sontay, North Vietnam prisoner-of-war commando raid. The show included a reading of the statements of the chairman of the Joint Chiefs of Staff and the delivery of a truckload of petitions on the prisoner-of-war issue. In a complaint to the FCC, the Student Association of the State University at Buffalo noted the above inconsistency in support of their censorship claim against ABC.[6]

ACTIVITIES

1. Find a long and important article in your school or daily newspaper, or tape a newscast of a major story. Then imagine that you are the editor of a weekly news summary and need to cut one-fourth of the article for space or time considerations. Mark the sentences or paragraphs that you think you can omit from the article and still tell the story completely and accurately.

2. Using the same story, cut one-fourth of it, this time omitting video segments, sentences, or paragraphs that make the summary more favorable to a person, group, or position than the original article (eliminate the negative, questionable, or unflattering statements included in the original). Finally, omit one-fourth of the story again, this time making the person, group, or position look worse than in the original by eliminating some of the favorable statements.

3. Select an important story in your school or daily newspaper, or tape a story covered in a newscast. Then go to the library and look up other daily newspapers of that same date to find how they covered the

story. Which paper had the more comprehensive coverage? Did the shorter article omit the unimportant or important parts of the story? Does the shorter version make any person, group, or position look better or worse than the longer version?

QUESTIONS FOR DISCUSSION

1. Can the public have any way of knowing that an important part of a story was deleted? If not, how can they be immune to the bias created by deletions?

2. If a citizen is suspicious that his newspaper might have deleted some important facts in its story of a particular event, how can he or she find other accounts of the same event? Do most citizens have the time to investigate such a deletion?

Generally, is the truth more likely to come out of three or four different versions of an event, compared for their consistency and facts, or from a single version of the event?

3. If you are sure that an editor deleted an important part of a story for political reasons, how could you prove it if he claims he deleted that part of the story because it wasn't important enough or that there wasn't enough space?

5

Selecting Photographs and Film

TEST CASE

The year: 1970. You are the managing editor of a large newspaper. One of your reporters has attended the three-day public testimony of more than forty Vietnam veterans in Washington, D.C. The veterans presented eyewitness accounts of atrocities committed by their units as a matter of policy. The inquiry, sponsored by the Citizens' Commission of Inquiry into U.S. War Crimes (an organization whose members include many Vietnam veterans), had the purpose of "exposing the U.S. military policies which inevitably result in war crimes like My Lai and [placing] responsiblity for these policies on those at the highest levels of military and civilian leadership." One of the veterans presented photographs he had personally taken. Among other atrocities, the slides showed an American GI cutting the ears from a Vietnamese corpse. The veteran testified that such mutilations were commonly employed as a means of proving "kills" and terrorizing the Vietnamese.

Compare your decision with the one that a major newspaper actually made in this situation.

The New York Times's news editor rejected the photographs because, as the reporter told one of the inquiry's organizers, they were too sensational and repulsive. Yet a few months later the Times printed a photograph of a group of East Pakistan rebels holding in their raised arms *the severed head of a West Pakistani soldier.*[1]

The New York Times also suppressed the first photograph of a Buddhist monk immolating himself in protest against the Saigon government. Later, when the Times's support of the war had cooled, they printed another photograph of a similar protest.[2]

Mark Davidson, a producer of television documentaries and news programs, has stated:

> Pictures always have exercised power that is unique: power to influence illiterates, seduce sophisticates, and manipulate the minds of everyone in between.

More people look at photographs than at anything else in newspapers and magazines. No single minor editorial decision is more important than that of selecting the photograph or film segment that the public will see. And yet this is an area where objectivity is hardest to achieve. If there is only space to use one, which of six photographs of a controversial figure is "objective": the one of him smiling, frowning, grimacing, talking, listening, or dozing? One editor may think the one of him smiling is most typical; another may think that the one of him dozing is more typical. Similarly, it is difficult to select photographs or film that "objectively" portray the real situation in a student-administration conflict, military conflict, or civil disturbance. One editor may select the film with the most violence and action as the best portrayal of the real situation; he may even use it because it is the most interesting or exciting. Another editor might think that a film showing peaceful negotiations is more appropriate, or more honest.

In making these difficult decisions, can an editor eliminate his own subjective impressions of what image is most representative? In the selection of a photograph or film segment, whether or not an editor is trying to be objective, trying to increase or decrease the dramatic and violent element, or trying purposely to enhance or discredit a person, group, activity, or cause, the selection will have some element of bias. This is understandable since there are so many pictures to choose from. Newspapers print fewer than 10 percent of the photographs available to them. Network evening newscasts use less than 5 percent of the available news film. The news consumer can't possibly know what photos or film footage weren't used (called "outtakes"), but he or she can try to be aware that another photograph of the same person or event might have created a different impression.

MEDIA DECISIONS

1. In his book *News from Nowhere,* Edward J. Epstein examined the editorial process by which news producers selected film for network news programs. He found that as a rule—no matter what the real situation was—producers tended to select pictures with dramatic action or violence.

However, he found that under certain circumstances, there were exceptions to this rule. In November 1968, Vietnam combat activity, U.S. deaths, and combat footage coming into the network newsrooms remained the same as they were the preceding year. Nevertheless, the producers cut down drastically on the amount of combat film selected for showing. An NBC producer explained that in his view the "story" was now negotiations, not combat. This coincided with President Johnson's halt of bombing over North Vietnam and his attempts to begin negotiations.

Another exception to the rule took place in April 1968, following the assassination of Martin Luther King, black civil rights leader. NBC selected film emphasizing the "relative quiet" and the "peaceful" situation in Harlem, when there were ample news films and wire service reports showing that the disturbances in 1968 were not peaceful at all, and in fact were as violent and destructive as the 1964 six-day New York City riots.[3]

2. A former editor of *American Legion Magazine* described how a "See It Now" television program in the 1950s used biased film selection in portraying a dispute between an American Legion post and members of the American Civil Liberties Union (ACLU):

Harsh lighting made the Legionnaires look ghastly, and their voices came through sounding harsh and unpleasant. The camera focused on a member of the color guard who had a small moustache, and when the colors were advanced, one sensed a disturbing resemblance to Hitler leading a corporal's guard of storm troopers—possibly because the sound of heels was amplified. When the cameras switched to the ACLU people in another part of the city, there was a tremendous difference. Soft lighting flattered the facial features. All these people looked like solid citizens, thoughtful and concerned about The Important Things. . . . What both groups said did not matter greatly. One could make up one's mind by the way they looked.[4]

3. The very conservative publisher of the Manchester, New Hampshire, *Union Leader*, William Loeb, apparently made sure his newspaper supported the candidate he favored for the Democratic party nomination in 1972. Loeb's choice, Los Angeles mayor Sam Yorty, received seventeen photographs, compared to ten for Edmund Muskie and four for Senator McGovern. The same study found that the paper used columnists, captions, headlines, and editorials to support the candidate Loeb favored.[5]

Time magazine selected twenty-one photographs of Dwight D. Eisenhower during thirteen weeks of the 1952 presidential campaign; all showed the candidate in a favorable light. During the same period, thirteen photographs of his opponent, Adlai Stevenson, were selected for publication. About half of these showed him in an unfavorable manner—eating, drinking, or grimacing.[6]

4. An NBC correspondent reporting on the 1970 election campaign in California said: "People are tired of being told that there are no simple answers to the complex problems of the world. So Ronald Reagan tells them there are simple answers. On campus unrest he says: 'If it takes a blood bath, then let's get it over with.'"

This narration was accompanied by a totally unrelated film segment showing Reagan at a firing range shooting a pistol at a target of a human figure.[7]

5. The decision to allocate money, talent, and resources to land a man on the moon has been seriously debated by scientists and politicians for many years. However, an examination of media coverage does not reveal this. During a two-month period in 1969, the *Los Angeles Times* and the *New York Times* had a total of fifty-one photographs on their front pages that were all either favorable or neutral toward the manned space program. At the same time there were no photographs giving attention to criticism of the basic decision to send a man to the moon or to criticism of the priority given to manned space flights.[8]

ACTIVITIES

1. Go through your collection of family photographs and select five that would most likely give a favorable impression of your family. Then select five that would most likely leave a viewer with a less favorable impression.

Briefly describe your family as depicted in the first selection. Then describe your family as depicted in the second selection.

2. Cut out all the photographs in your daily newspaper. Take them with you to the library to compare them with the photographs in a different daily newspaper. For each paper note how many photographs are from the wire service, how many from the paper's own photographers, and how many are not identified as to source.

Briefly describe the differences between the two newspapers' selection of photographs.

3. Go through your daily newspaper or news magazine and classify each photograph as a favorable or unfavorable depiction of the subject. Add a short explanation of why you think it is so. Videotape a television newscast and make the same kind of classification.

QUESTIONS FOR DISCUSSION

1. Are pictures of manned space flight or of a politician neutral just because the pictures are not obviously favorable or unfavorable? Is the mere publication or airing of such film or photos an advantage to the space program or to a politician? Because dissent against the manned space program produces few spectacular events compared to a moon landing, is that a justification for photographically ignoring dissent? What kind of photographs could depict dissent?

2. Is it more advantageous for a politician to have a favorable photograph of himself on the front page or to have a favorable comment on the editorial page?

3. How do the elements of film such as lighting, relative size, framing, and focus affect the depiction of the subject matter and the viewer's response? Can a film be shot or edited to make the image of a person communicate a visual message that contradicts what the person is saying, or that enhances what the person is saying?

6

Placement

TEST CASE

The year: 1972. You are the news editor of a daily newspaper. On what page would you place the following news item?

A government report made public today called alcohol the nation's greatest drug problem, warping nine million lives and costing about $15 billion a year. It said alcohol was the cause of almost half of all arrests in the United States and of 28,000 highway automobile deaths. The report added that abusers of alcohol shorten their life-span by 10 to 12 years, and their lost work time costs about $10 billion. The welfare, health, and property damage resulting from alcohol abuse costs another $5 billion. The report has the authority of a government publication and for the first time brings together a substantial portion of current knowledge on the consequences of using alcohol.[1]

Compare your decision with the one that three newspapers actually made in this situation.

The Honolulu Star-Bulletin *placed this story on page 16 of section II. The* Chicago Tribune *placed it at the bottom of page 4. The* New York Times *placed it on the top of page 1.*

People tend to assume that just because a story leads off the evening newscast or is placed on the front page, it is significant and deserves to be there. Similarly, if an item appears on the back page or is given a few seconds on the tail end of a newscast, people assume for this reason alone that the item is not too significant. Placement not only confers on a story a degree of relative importance, it determines how many people will even find out about the story. A story on front pages across the nation will be read by millions more people than a story placed in the back pages.

It is difficult for an editor to be objective in his placement decisions. Even traditional professional standards for decision making may contain a hidden bias (for example, the idea that political stories are more important than social or environmental stories). One editor may quite honestly think that a story belongs on page 1 while another editor may be equally sincere in thinking the story belongs in the back pages. Each editor may be able to defend his placement and news standards adequately.

Other editors may consciously use a personal, subjective standard for placement. Such an editor may place an article on the back pages because he doesn't want the public to notice it or think it is important. Or, he may put on page 1 a story that favors a friend or a special crusade.

Regardless of the editor's motive, the news consumer would do well to ask himself whether any story could or should have been placed in a more important position.

MEDIA DECISIONS

1. A group of wealthy millionaire oilmen, defense contractors, and real estate executives gave Richard Nixon $18,000 to help pay his expenses as a congressman. This story was one of the top ten stories of 1952 as selected by newspaper editors. Yet out of 70 news-

papers in 48 different states, only 7 chose to place the story on the front page the first chance they had. Two out of the 7 printed the response of the Nixon camp without reference to the original story. All 5 of the Los Angeles dailies kept the story on the inside pages during the first two days.[2]

2. From 1938 through 1953, the *New York Times* printed twenty-six news stories that persuasively linked cigarette smoking with cancer and shortening of life. The *Times* printed none of these on the front page.[3]

3. Campaigning for the presidential nomination in 1960—eight years before hunger in America became an important issue—Senator John F. Kennedy made a speech in which he made the following allegations:

> The facts are that 17,000,000 Americans go to bed hungry every night. Fifteen million Americans live in substandard housing. Seven million Americans are struggling to survive on an income of less than $2,000 a year.[4]

The *New York Times* placed this article in the middle of page 16 with a small headline. Of three network radio newscasts, Peter Hackes on NBC, Lowell Thomas on CBS, and Edward P. Morgan on ABC, only Morgan mentioned Kennedy's statement.

4. During the campaign in the autumn of 1972, Democratic party vice-presidential candidate Sargent Shriver charged that President Nixon "had peace in his lap" early in 1969 but "blew" the opportunity offered by the North Vietnamese. This charge produced responses from former high-ranking officials. Averell Harriman and Cyrus Vance, President Johnson's negotiators at the Paris peace talks in 1968, supported Shriver's charge. The *New York Times* headlined their support on page 1.

The next day, Henry Cabot Lodge, the negotiator President Nixon chose to succeed Vance and Harriman, stated: "I can state categorically and unequivocally that I neither was informed of any such peace opportunity nor had any reason to believe one existed." The *Times* printed Lodge's position on page 18 in the twenty-first paragraph of a story headlined: MCGOVERN ACCUSES NIXON OF A 'LOW ROAD' CAMPAIGN.

A few days later, Dean Rusk, who was secretary of state when Harriman, Vance, and Shriver (as ambassador) were in Paris, said that he saw no hint of a signal from the North Vietnamese that they were ready to make peace. The *Times* placed this story on page 25.[5]

5. A team of psychologists sponsored by the office of the surgeon general of the United States found that

> at least under some circumstances, repeated exposure to televised aggression can lead children to accept what they have seen as a partial guide for their own actions. As a result, the present entertainment offerings of the television medium may be contributing, in some measure, to the aggressive behavior of many normal children.[6]

These findings were later included in the final report by the surgeon general's Advisory Committee on Television and Social Behavior, made public in early 1972. (See test case, Chapter 2.)

The *Los Angeles Examiner* placed this article on the top of page 1 with an eight-column banner headline.

The *New York Times* placed it on page 45.

The *Chicago Tribune* didn't print the story.[7]

ACTIVITIES

1. Go through your daily newspaper and select ten stories that you would put on the front page if you were the news editor. List the stories in sequence from

one to ten according to how much prominence you would give them on page 1. Briefly, explain why you think each story is important.

2. Using papers from three consecutive days, select from the front pages six articles that you think are so trivial or unimportant that they deserve to be on the back pages or not even printed at all. Briefly explain why you think these stories are unimportant. Explain why you think the editor placed them on page 1.

3. Compare the front pages of two different newspapers published the same morning. Which paper do you think made the best placement decisions? Why?

QUESTIONS FOR DISCUSSION

1. What are some of the favorable advantages to a person, group, or cause if they are favorably described in an article on page 1; if they are critically described? How different would it be if the same article were placed on the bottom of page 35?

2. How is it possible to prove that a certain newspaper is placing important articles on back pages for partisan rather than journalistic reasons? If it can't be proved, why not?

3. If people's ideas about what happens in the world comes from their newspaper, will readers of two very different newspapers have significantly different ideas about what happens?

Is an event unimportant unless the newspapers or television notice it?

7

Journalists at Work

TEST CASE

The year: 1971. You are a reporter covering Bob Hope's Christmas show at Long Binh, Vietnam. The following three events occurred:

1. Martha Raye got a standing ovation when she told the GIs that antiwar demonstrators back home "aren't even fit to shine your boots."

2. The show was picketed by GIs carrying signs that read "Where is Jane Fonda?" (an antiwar activist and actress).

3. During the performance a group of military police came on stage with a banner reading "Pigs for Peace."

Which one or two events will you emphasize?

Compare your decision with the one that two reporters actually made in this situation.

The Chicago Tribune reporter emphasized the "thunderous standing ovation" that Martha Raye received.

A New Statesman reporter emphasized that the stadium was picketed by GIs with the Jane Fonda signs, and that a group of military police mounted the stage with their banner.[1]

Assuming a reporter has a choice and isn't assigned a specific story, the selection of one of many possible

49

stories is only the first decision he makes. He then must decide, because of space or time considerations, to discard some of his facts. As a former editor of the *New York Times* put it:

> The reporter, the most objective reporter, collects fifty facts. Out of the fifty he selects twelve to include in his story. Thus he discards thirty-eight.
>
> Then the reporter . . . decides which of the facts shall be the first paragraph of the story, thus emphasizing one fact above the other eleven.[2]

A reporter must also decide whom to interview and how much of the interview to include. He has to decide how reliable his sources of information are and which facts need further verification. After making all these decisions, he must be sure that he keeps his own viewpoint out of the story; his own opinion must be labeled as such and set apart from his news reports.

The newscaster broadcasts the news that reporters have written or filmed, but he must decide what tone of voice, inflection, pauses, facial expressions, and posture to use. In so doing, he communicates his attitude about the news stories. Even no change in facial expression or tone, as he goes from telling about a sports event to an atrocity, is communicating an attitude. Research done by a leading psychologist reveals that of the total message of approval communicated by a broadcaster, only 7 percent is communicated by words while 93 percent is communicated by vocal and facial expressions.[3] Some facial expressions are so fleeting that we can't see them, but they register on the subconscious. Such expressions can be observed in slow motion.[4]

The commentator or columnist has more freedom than either the reporter or the newscaster—and probably more influence. He decides what issue he will comment on, what viewpoint to adopt, and what facts and style of presentation are relevant to the topic. He can use poetry, philosophy, analogy, irony, or ridicule.

The network commentaries are often placed in the crucial position of ending a newscast where they serve to summarize, relate, or give order to previous news items. This imparts to the audience an attitude into which they can fit the previously unrelated news events. If the commentators choose to support a policy in this way they can give that policy a decided advantage.

Like the reporter, the cameraman and photographer have to make important decisions. If a cameraman or sound man is limited to, or decides to record, only five minutes of an hour's speech or demonstration, he must decide which five minutes gets to the essence of the event. California Governor Ronald Reagan said that by watching when the cameras were rolling, he could tell what the cameramen "have decided they will let the public see." [5]

The cameraman may have been ordered to film only five minutes, and he may have filmed them not with the intention of making the governor look bad or good, but with the intention of getting the most lively moments. Nevertheless, the governor is right; the people will see only what the cameraman films. And those few moments may give an unfavorable portrait of the governor while his better moments were not filmed at all.

The news consumer should always keep in mind that many activities or moments are not reported at all, and that different reporters, newscasters, or cameramen—because of their selectivity and emphasis—can depict the same event in very different ways.

MEDIA DECISIONS

1. Reporters for network television have the task of covering the statements of important people regarding controversial issues. Analysis of these selections indicates that sometimes reporters allow their personal bias to influence their choices of whom to interview.

A 1968 analysis of the partisan selection of opinion showed that at all three national networks the reporters selected opinions that were weighted against Richard Nixon, George Wallace, the white middle class, and supporters of the Vietnam War.[6]

2. Reporters are often under pressure to produce stories in a hurry so that they can both meet the news agencies' deadlines and beat other reporters to a story. As a result, many fail to take on the responsibility of verifying the facts they have obtained.

In July 1972, columnist Jack Anderson did not take the necessary steps to verify his claim that vice-presidential nominee Senator Thomas Eagleton had been arrested for drunk driving. Anderson's accusations proved false; Eagleton had never been arrested on such a charge. Anderson, in admitting his error, claimed that it was the journalistic competition to come up first with a big story that prompted him to print the story before taking on the responsibility of verifying the information. An Associated Press study found that only fifteen of fifty newspapers that placed the story on page 1 also placed the correction on page 1.

3. Opinions, commentaries, and editorials are supposed to be labeled as such. To insert them into a straight news report is considered unprofessional and unethical since it slants the news and gives an advantage to one side of a controversy under a pretense of neutrality. Nevertheless, many reporters insert their opinions into the straight news so subtly that the audience is seldom able to recognize the opinion.

The following statements are examples of hidden opinions that were inserted into straight news reports:

a. An NBC correspondent wrapped up a report detailing inferior medical care for minority groups by saying, "The problem of bad and expensive medical care cannot be cured quickly by some big government program." [7]

b. A CBS correspondent interjected this phrase in

his report from Vietnam: "Even though Ho [Ho
Chi Minh, former president of North Vietnam]
is the man responsible for fifteen years of war
there." [8]

c. A CBS correspondent in the Mideast ended his
report about Russian-Arab relations by saying,
"But of course sound argument has not always
dictated Arab behavior." [9]

d. Shortly after U.S. and South Vietnamese troops
moved into Cambodia in 1970, President Nixon
presided over a series of briefings in which he
explained the purpose of the action to congressional leaders. Reporting on the event, a CBS
correspondent described the sessions as "a dialogue of the deaf." [10]

4. Eric Sevareid took a total of ten minutes on the
"Walter Cronkite" newscast to give four different commentaries favorable to the manned space program
during a two-month period in 1969. He gave no commentary against the program nor did any other CBS
commentator. One of his commentaries went so far
as to deny that the other side of the argument had
any substance:

All arguments, sociological arguments, philosophical
arguments we've heard and talked about for weeks
and months and years—should we do this instead of
something else—somehow they all vanish in a cloud of
smoke. This can be done and therefore it's done.
There really isn't any argument.[11]

5. A former actor who became governor of California, Ronald Reagan, was very conscious of what an
anchor man can say with nonverbal gestures. Reagan
told a group of television executives that he knows
from experience that a news commentator, using facial
expression, can in effect "call the governor a liar" as
he quotes what the governor said. "The inflection
of the announcer's voice, the arched eyebrows, the

skeptical expression, all these," the governor said, "can and have injected an element of bias in television news." [12]

ACTIVITIES RELATED TO REPORTING
AND PHOTOGRAPHY

1. Choose an issue, group, or person in your school or community as the subject for a factual news story. In writing the story, be as objective as possible: use verifiable information and statements from various sources, but don't use your own opinions.

After gathering the facts decide which half of them are important enough to go into your story and which half to exclude. Write a 300- to 400-word story.

Rewrite the story, this time purposely selecting and excluding facts in order to create a favorable impression of the person, group, or one side of the issue. Do not actually express your own opinion or approval; let the selection and placement of facts make the subject or argument look good. Do not use false or imagined information.

Write the story a third time, using facts and statements to create an impression unfavorable to that same person, group, or side of the issue.

2. Using a still, motion-picture, or video camera, take no more than five photographs or three minutes of film depicting a person or group in your school or community. Try to have your photographs, film, or videotape capture the most typical or important characteristics or actions of the person or group.

Cover the same topic with photographs, film, or tape that will make the person or group look good or admirable.

Cover the topic a third time, purposely taking photographs, film, or videotape that will make the person or group look bad, silly, or despicable.

3. Cut out all the photographs on the first three pages of your daily newspaper. Under each, describe a different type of photograph that could have been used to accompany the story. Videotape a story on a newscast or sportscast and describe a different kind of videotape segment that could have been used in its place.

QUESTIONS FOR DISCUSSION

1. Does a reporter or cameraman have to lie, use trickery, or misquote a person in order to produce a favorable or unfavorable bias, or can the mere selection of detail and style of writing produce a bias? Which is the more effective bias, one that is produced by the presentation of false information or one that is produced without violating any professional journalistic standards? (Does your answer differ depending on whether the readers have access to only one source of information or to many sources?)

2. Just because a cameraman or reporter tries his best to be objective and fair, does this mean that his photographs or story will be objective or fair?

3. If all the reporters on a newspaper are liberal, or all are conservative, will their selection of stories and facts produce an overall bias supporting their political philosophy? Or can their attempts to be objective produce an overall neutral newspaper favoring no political viewpoint?

ACTIVITIES RELATED TO COMMENTATORS AND NEWSCASTERS

1. Watch a network evening news program and pay particular attention to the commentary. Tape it if you can. Then write a commentary of your own on the

same topic, but one that has just the opposite mesage or attitude toward the subject. Feel free to quote from famous people, and to use poems, analogies, and similes.

2. Select the newscaster on a local television station who you think most uses facial expressions and tone of voice to communicate an attitude toward events he is reporting. Choose a news story about a controversial event like a demonstration and report the story as you think he would by mimicking his style.

3. Select a news story of a controversial event or statement made by a politician. Report the event three times. First, use facial expressions and voice qualities that show approval and respect. Second, use similar nonverbal expressions to show disapproval, contempt, or ridicule. Third, report the story objectively. Use the class as audience, or videotape your performance.

QUESTIONS FOR DISCUSSION

1. If a news program has the same commentator or commentators night after night, is this fair to all political viewpoints?

2. How is it possible to make the commentary section of a news program fair to all viewpoints?

3. Is it possible for a newscaster to avoid or eliminate nonverbal expressions as he reports the news? How can the bias created by the newscaster's nonverbal expressions be counteracted or balanced?

4. Is an expressionless face dressed in a suit and tie a form of bias in itself?

Books for Further Study

Aronson, James. *Deadline for the Media: Today's Challenges to Press, TV, and Radio.* New York: Bobbs-Merrill, 1972. The growing movement of journalists who demand more editorial power—from a very liberal-radical viewpoint.

Dinsmore, Herman H. *All the News That Fits.* New Rochelle, N.Y.: Arlington House, 1969. A study of bias in the *New York Times*—from a very conservative viewpoint.

Epstein, Edward J. *News from Nowhere: Television and the News.* New York: Random House, 1973. How the processes and structure of network news organizations influence the news.

Hayakawa, S. I., ed. *The Use and Misuse of Language.* Greenwich, Conn.: Fawcett World Library, 1962.

Hohenberg, John. *The News Media: A Journalist Looks at His Profession.* New York: Holt, Rinehart, and Winston, 1968.

Postman, Neil, Weingartner, Charles, and Moran, Terence, eds. *Language in America.* Indianapolis, Ind.: Pegasus, 1969. Readings on the use and misuse of language by politicians, bureaucrats, censors, advertisers, educators, economists, psychologists, and lovers.

II

CENSORSHIP—AS DEFINED
BY THE CONSUMER

When people talk of censorship they are often referring to outright government censorship of newspapers, television, radio, movies, or books—a situation that prevails in nondemocratic countries.

Democratic countries usually have laws that make it difficult or impossible for the government to resort to outright censorship of the press. In the United States this protection is built right into our Constitution. The First Amendment states: "Congress shall make no law . . . abridging the freedom of speech, or of the press."

But governments are not the only organizations that try to censor information; the press itself can do so for one reason or another—and there is no law restricting them.

A reporter may spend months researching, investigating, and writing an important story, but it won't reach anyone if an editor or publisher refuses to print the story. A hard-hitting documentary won't expose anything or inform the public if a network or station executive decides it's too controversial to show. An organization or group of citizens might save thousands of dollars in order to produce an advertisement, documentary, or program they would like the American people to see, but it won't do them any good if networks or stations refuse to allow them to buy time to present it.

Journalists and broadcast executives may not want to consider their actions as censorship because they claim there are professional reasons for depriving the people of certain stories or programs. They may claim that a documentary or program doesn't come up to their journalistic standards of objectivity, fairness, or responsibility. Rare is the journalist or media executive who will admit to censoring information for purely personal or political reasons.

On the other hand, a news consumer might think such decisions should be defined as censorship, for, regardless of the news standards or motive, important information and viewpoints are being kept from him. This is why a consumer's definition of censorship should expand to include journalistic judgments as well as (in the conventional definition) the more deliberate suppression of information for personal, political, obscenity, or national security considerations.

It is very difficult to determine the motives of those who suppress information. For this reason, evil motives do not need to be proven before an editorial or decision-making process can be considered censorship from a consumer's standpoint.

Even if some forms of censorship are only resorted to infrequently, this in no way decreases the danger of censorship. A small amount of critical information could make the the difference between life and death for a person or a country, or cause a large number of people to modify or question their attitudes toward a policy or person.

CENSORSHIP—AS DEFINED BY THE CONSUMER

formality, and broadcast executives may not want
to saddle their actions as "censorship" because they
think there are professional reasons for depriving the
people of certain stories or programs. They may claim

8

Censorship of Major Stories

TEST CASE

*The year: 1969. You are the editor in chief of a large-
circulation magazine. A literary agent offers you a sensational story by a Vietnam veteran telling of events in
the village of My Lai on 16 March 1968, when American
soldiers killed hundreds of defenseless women, children,
and old people. Another free-lance writer offers you a
story about the same event. Both appear to be well-
researched and responsible articles.*

*Are you going to print the story and be the first news
agency to inform the public about this event though it
might lessen public support for the U.S. war effort and
displease the Pentagon? If you decide to refuse the story,
will you assign one of your reporters to investigate the
alleged atrocities and print whatever he discovers?*

**Compare your decision with the one that many news
agencies actually made in this situation.**

Life, Look, Newsweek, Harper's, *United Press International, Associated Press, one network, and major newspapers in Boston and New York refused an offer of the
story by a literary agent. Ramparts magazine's bid for the
story was rejected by the author, Ron Ridenhour, because
he didn't want the story associated with a radical magazine. Seymour Hersh's story of the same event was also
rejected by several publications including Life and Look.
He finally sold the story to Dispatch News Service which
released the story on 13 November 1969. After the story
broke, nearly every news agency, including those who

had originally refused it, gave the story prominent coverage.[1]

The government may ask or exert pressure to force newspapers to censor certain stories because, in its view, they contain secret information that could jeopardize national security if found out by the enemy. This could be information about troop movements, plans to invade or overthrow another government, or secret negotiations. It could also be information that might cause the American people or other countries to question the sincerity of past or present government leaders.

Media owners have usually agreed with the government's reasoning and have censored such stories on their own, or at the government's request, believing that to do so was in the public interest. But on a few occasions newspapers have refused the government's request and printed a story anyway. They explained that in their own judgment the information involved was not vital to national security and that the national interest and American lives were better protected by informing the people.

Citizens should not automatically accept the government's idea of what would jeopardize national security *or* a news agency's idea of what the national interest is. In cases when censorship does not appear to be justified, the news consumer should hope that at least one of the major news agencies covers the story. This will usually nullify the censorship of others by forcing them to finally cover the story or lose credibility with the public.

MEDIA DECISIONS

1. Late in 1960, the editors of the *Nation* magazine sent to all major news agencies an article detailing

how the United States was well on its way to sponsoring an invasion of Cuba without a declaration of war. The *Nation*'s story was rejected by seventy-five major news agencies. One newspaper, the *Gazette and Daily* of York, Pennsylvania, printed it. Four months later in April, ten days before the invasion actually took place, the *New York Times* finally printed the story, but only after top management gave orders to play down the story and omit the most vital elements. The *Times* justified its treatment of the article by claiming it was in the national interest to do so. They claimed that publicizing such information would have alerted the enemy and thereby endangered the lives of the men involved.[2]

2. In 1965, the United States increased the role of U.S. ground troops in Vietnam to such an extent that it amounted to a major offensive buildup and a significant change in policy. The American public was told that the troops were merely a small defensive and support force. Max Frankel, Diplomatic Correspondent of the *New York Times*, said that the *Times* knew the deployment of troops was a major offensive move, but concealed this information from the public because they felt it might have triggered an agreement between Russia and China to intervene in the war. Since this, according to Frankel, might have caused a major international conflict, the *Times* felt it was in the national interest to keep the information secret.[3]

3. In August 1972, *Ramparts* magazine published startling information about the U.S. National Security Agency. Written by a former member of the NSA, the article revealed that the NSA's electronic outposts around the world are able to monitor all Russian communications, break their codes, and thus keep track of every Russian bomber, missile, and submarine as well as the movements of important diplomats and generals. If true, this vast superiority in electronic technology gives the United States a decided military advantage over Russia.

Ramparts sent out advance copies of the article to eight news agencies. The *New York Times*, Reuters news service, and *Newsday* all took the lead and printed their own story about the revelations. *Time* and *Newsweek* completely ignored the lead. Both the *Washington Post* and the *Boston Globe* assigned reporters to investigate the revelations, but later killed their own reporters' stories. The *St. Louis Post-Dispatch* ignored *Ramparts*'s advance copy and merely printed the story as it came out over the *New York Times* wire service.[4]

4. Late in 1972, two university students answered an advertisement in the *Chicago Tribune* asking for Russian linguists. The students found that their job would be to attend a Latin American university while they translated tapes of conversations bugged at the Russian embassy in the country where they would be acting as students.

When the students suspected the job really involved the Central Intelligence Agency, they reported the story to *Parade* magazine. *Parade* attempted to confirm their allegations. In response to *Parade*'s inquiries, the CIA said it wouldn't be in the national interest to expose this CIA cover and suggested that the patriotic thing would be to censor the story. *Parade* disagreed with the CIA's idea of patriotism and printed it anyway.

In advance of publication, *Parade* sent copies of the article to the wire services, the *New York Times*, the *Washington Post*, the *Los Angeles Times*, and others. None of them followed up or reported on the story.[5]

5. In June 1971, the *New York Times* published part of a top secret Pentagon study called the "Pentagon Papers." The papers were made available by Daniel Ellsberg, a Vietnam veteran and former Pentagon researcher. The Pentagon had had the study made in order to understand the decision-making process involving U.S. policy in Vietnam.

Among other disclosures, the documents revealed that the U.S. government had from the beginning purposely deceived the American people about the real reasons for the United States intervention in Vietnam and about the true U.S. role and military strategy in that country.

The Nixon administration asked the *Times* to stop publication. In refusing, the *Times* stated: "It is in the interest of the people of this country to be informed of the material contained in this series of articles." The Justice Department then quickly asked for and got a court order restraining the *Times* from printing the remainder of the documents.

The *Washington Post*, followed shortly after by the *Boston Globe*, the *Christian Science Monitor*, the *St. Louis Post-Dispatch*, and thirteen other papers, continued where the *Times* had left off. Some of them later faced court restraining orders also, but by this time the essence of the documents was revealed to the public.

The Supreme Court finally ruled that the *Times* had a right to publish the papers because the administration had failed to show that their publication would constitute a grave and immediate danger to national security. The Court stated that if the administration could have proven such a threat, then it would have had a right to get an injunction preventing publication.

A week after the *Times* was ordered by the lower court to stop publication, a *Newsweek* opinion poll showed that 48 percent of the public were against the government's attempt to censor the *Times*, 33 percent approved, and 19 percent had no opinion.[6]

ACTIVITIES

1. Imagine you are the editor of your school newspaper and have received reliable and verifiable information that part of the student-body funds, designated

for the improvement of the public-address system for rock music at noontime, have, instead, been spent to improve the public-address system at the football field. If publicized, the story may embarrass the principal, a coach, members of the student council, and the school as a whole.

While you print this story?

Write a brief statement justifying your decision.

2. Suppose that a Latin American country has recently changed governments. The first move of the new government was to confiscate all United States–owned businesses in their country including a broadcasting station that you partially owned.

You are also the publisher of an important daily newspaper in the United States and have just received reliable top secret information that the United States plans to invade this country without a declaration of war or public debate. The purpose of the invasion is to topple the new government. If successful, the invasion would restore your ownership of the station.

Will you print the information about the invasion plans? Justify your decision, paying particular attention to the secrecy of the information, the public's rights to be informed, the national interest, and the Constitution.

3. Imagine that you are the editor of your school paper and have received indisputable information revealing that your local daily paper has given press cards to plainclothes police detectives. Posing as newspapermen, they can get more information about a radical group they are investigating. The chief of police has admitted that the story is true. But he also has requested that you not print anything about it because it will handicap the police. The chief claims that this is in the town's and school's interest since he suspects the group may be plotting to bomb the school.

If you decide to print the story, write a letter to the chief explaining why you are refusing his request.

If you agree to censor the story, assume that the

police later arrest some members of the group for conspiracy. In the court case that follows, it is revealed that the policemen gained the confidence of the group because they were accepted as sympathetic reporters. How might this revelation damage your newspaper's capacity to report on this type of organization in the future?

QUESTIONS FOR DISCUSSION

1. Is it in the national interest for a news agency to censor information about the secret movement of U.S. troops in their planned invasion of another country if neither the Congress nor the people have been asked to approve of the invasion?

2. Is it possible for everyone to agree on what the national interest is in every case, or is it possible that different citizens and editors can honestly disagree about it? Who should be the final judge?

3. Can a policy be established whereby the public's right to information is not sacrificed by government and mass media secrecy or censorship? Will this policy guarantee the government enough secrecy for effective functioning and carrying out of delicate negotiations with foreign countries?

9

Censorship of Documentaries

TEST CASE

The year: 1967. You are the top executive of a network news operation that has financed a documentary about deplorable prison conditions and the individual plight of prisoners facing the death penalty. A preview showing drew praise from television critics. However, the documentary is very hard-hitting and you feel it may antagonize some politicians and prison officials who might consider the program too one-sided.

Will you show this documentary or will you censor it?

Compare your decision with the one that the networks actually made in this situation.

For three years ABC refused to show "Death Row, USA," produced by author Truman Capote. When it was offered for sale, neither CBS nor NBC showed any interest in buying it.[1]

When an article or book exposes wrongdoing or brings to light a neglected problem, it often has little effect on public attitudes or on politicians. When the same story is made into a documentary and shown on network television during prime time, it can have profound repercussions. Public opinion is modified, politicians take a stand, and the government agency or corporation involved takes corrective action—or counterattacks against the network.

When Senator J. William Fulbright's book *The Pentagon Propaganda Machine* was published in 1970, there was little response. But later when CBS aired "The Selling of the Pentagon," a documentary based in large part on the book, the repercussions were enormous. The Pentagon criticized the program as being journalistically dishonest, but it also stopped some of its more questionable propaganda activities. And both the public and congressmen were made more aware of what a large-scale propaganda operation they were subsidizing.

Similarly, there were articles from 1965 to 1968 that told of hunger and malnutrition affecting millions of Americans. Yet this situation did not become a major issue until CBS's "Hunger in America" was shown on prime time television in 1968. The Department of Agriculture responded immediately by expanding its food program to include forty-two more countries, increasing the monthly surplus of food going to the poor, and calling for the expansion of the food-stamp program.

The executive judgments that determine whether the public will see a documentary are based on financial considerations, professional journalistic standards, and perhaps on a fear that someone will require free time to answer under the Fairness Doctrine (see Chapters 19 and 20). A rejection can also occur because of personal or political considerations.

In addition, individual broadcast executives will differ in their judgments because their standards vary. What a network will reject, a local station might show. On another occasion, what a network will show might be rejected by a local station. Whatever the professional standards or motives involved, it is obvious that the censorship of a controversial documentary is a matter that seriously affects the public interest as well as each individual's right to be informed.

MEDIA DECISIONS

1. In 1968, the Columbia University Center for Mass Communications offered all three networks a documentary depicting the horrifying effects of the atomic bomb on individual Japanese victims. At the Japanese government's insistence, the U.S. Army had released the film after suppressing it for twenty-three years. Professor Sumner J. Glimcher of Columbia University described the film as "perhaps the best argument for people to live in peace." All three networks told Columbia University they weren't interested in showing it. None of them used the army's available film to produce a documentary of their own. In late 1970, the Public Broadcasting Service showed the film.[2]

2. "The Race for Space," produced by an independent producer in 1960, was turned down by all three networks even though it had a willing sponsor. The networks, who were working on similar documentaries, based their rejection on a policy of "responsibility," claiming that the only way they could meet their standards of objectivity, fairness, and responsibility was to reject all outside productions and show only those produced by their own staffs. Many independent stations did show "The Race for Space."[3]

Other "Outside" productions refused by all three networks have included: "Primary," a highly praised documentary covering the 1960 Democratic party presidential primary battle between Senator John F. Kennedy and Hubert Humphrey;[4] a proposed debate between Russian Premier Nikita Khrushchev and four American graduate students in 1960;[5] and a 1969 program that was to present Secretary of Defense Melvin Laird debating young activists on what would happen in the event of an invasion of Cambodia.[6]

3. The Public Broadcasting Service (PBS) determines which programs will be shown over public tele-

vision's network of over two hundred stations. In 1971, it ordered National Educational Television to censor from its regularly produced program, "The Great American Dream Machine," a documentary segment reporting on the FBI. Through interviews with former FBI agents, the report showed how undercover men infiltrated radical new left groups with the purpose of provoking incidents that would give law officials an excuse to move in and make arrests. Music was substituted for the censored report.[7]

An overwhelming majority of local station managers endorsed the authority of PBS's board of directors to censor such productions.[8]

4. "Survival of Spaceship Earth," a documentary aimed at increasing the environmental awareness in underdeveloped countries, was independently produced in Hollywood at a cost of $775,000, a sum provided by five foundations. It was shown in Europe in 1972 and received Sweden's highest recognition, the Vasa Award. CBS, among others, refused to show the documentary. It was later aired by an independent television station in Los Angeles.[9]

All three networks refused to show the official film version of the report of the Presidential Commission on Population Growth and the American Future. The report emphasized the environmental effects of overpopulation and advocated legalized abortion, but it covered both pro and con positions. The Public Broadcasting Service later aired it in November 1972.

The networks' decisions in both cases were no doubt influenced by the fact that these two documentaries were controversial and were produced by people outside the networks. ABC rejected the report on overpopulation because of their policy of rejecting documentaries that "push a particular point of view." [10]

5. ABC News let its principal sponsors of news documentaries determine which topics would merit production. After being given a list of topics by ABC,

the sponsors—through their advertising agency—would select the topics and even suggest some of their own, some of which were accepted by ABC. The sponsors had a tendency to shy away from controversial topics and instead select "cultural" or industrial-type documentaries. In 1970, for example, Minnesota Mining and Manufacturing chose to sponsor "The Golden Age of the Automobile," "The Westerners," "The Unseen World," "The Great Barrier Reef," "The Golden Age of the Railroad," and "The Congo River."

North American (a space contractor) had previously chosen to sponsor "The View from Space," a program that argued both visually and verbally for a continuation of the manned space program beyond the moon landing. B. F. Goodrich (a defense contractor) chose in 1966 and in 1967 to sponsor ABC News documentaries on Vietnam that were produced with Pentagon cooperation.

The sponsors often kept in close touch during production, and at times examined scripts and editing. On occasion, this involvement led to alteration of a program's content.[11]

ACTIVITIES

1. Discover a condition, situation, or practice in your school or community that you think is intolerable for one reason or another. Plan how you would go about making a half-hour radio or television documentary that would expose the situation and deal with causes, responsibilities, and remedies.

On the left-hand side of a large piece of paper, list in sequence the people you might interview and the kind of information you might need for the narration. On the right-hand side, describe briefly the things you would record or film to go along with the narration. If you are doing a radio documentary, use the right-hand side to describe any sound effects you would use.

If time and equipment are available, begin gathering information and film or videotape footage for a documentary that you can present in class.

2. Do you think some of the people covered in your proposed documentary might not want the sound tape, film, or videotape to be played or shown? Assume that you couldn't get their cooperation in your attempts to take film or gather information; could you still proceed?

Briefly write what you think their objections would be. How would you answer their objections?

If some people asked you not to show the documentary because they thought that it might embarrass important people or that it was unfair, would you show it anyway? Why?

3. List any topics that might lend themselves to a controversial documentary exposing powerful national interests—the kind of report the networks might shy away from or haven't yet made.

QUESTIONS FOR DISCUSSION

1. Do you agree with the network policy of not showing documentaries—even good ones—produced by people outside their own news departments? Why? Is the public generally aware when a proposed documentary has been rejected or when one already made has been censored?

2. If, in addition to the moderate networks, there were a network of a radical-left orientation and one of a radical-right orientation, would there be a better chance of all documentaries finding a willing broadcaster? Why or why not?

3. What purpose does "investigative" journalism

(the search for and exposure of the underlying causes, story, or corruption) serve besides creating sensational news and selling more papers? Can there be too many hard-hitting documentaries on television, even if they are good and the problems they deal with are real?

10

Censorship of Network Productions

TEST CASE

The year: 1971. You are a station manager of a local television station affiliated with the CBS network. The network is offering a news special, "The Selling of the Pentagon," that exposes the numerous propaganda techniques and strategies used by the Pentagon to gain public support for its policies and activities. You feel it is a good documentary on a topic that is seldom covered, yet it is very controversial and is sure to bring an angry response from the Pentagon and the federal government

Will you carry this documentary?

Compare your decision with the one that some affiliates actually made in this situation.

Thirty-nine of CBS's 204 affiliate stations did not air "The Selling of the Pentagon" when it was first offered.[1]

Federal communications law prohibits a network from owning more than five television stations. As a result, only fifteen of the nearly six hundred commercial television network activities are owned by the networks (ABC, NBC, CBS). The rest are owned by other companies or individuals. The fifteen network-owned stations usually show all network-produced documentaries and public-affairs programs, but about 25 percent of such programs are turned down by independently owned affiliates.[2] Since by law the affiliates —not the networks—are held responsible for programming in the public interest, they retain the authority to reject such programs. There are five reasons why affiliates reject network documentaries and public-affairs programs.

The first is financial. Since the airing of a network documentary or public-affairs program may not bring in as much advertising money as a program scheduled by the local station—such as a movie—it may be rejected or shown in another time slot. However, the station may feel in certain cases that its moral, professional, and legal obligation to serve the public interest demands that they show the program, even at a financial loss.

Second, a rejection may be based on the owner's fear that the program may antagonize the audience, local organizations, and advertisers.

Third, a station may judge that the documentary does not meet the station's journalistic standards of objectivity, fairness, or responsibility.

Fourth, the station may fear that it will receive demands for free time from groups who think the documentary unfair to their position. The station may also fear that the federal government, through its influence on the FCC, may make it difficult for them to get a license renewal if programs are shown that are critical of government policy or actions. In late 1972, the director of White House telecommunications policy, Clay Whitehead, gave a speech in which he encouraged affiliates to be on the lookout for, and reject, network productions that have what he termed a liberal "ideological plugola" and "elitist gossip" that is habitually critical of the administration. He also cautioned local noncommercial stations to beware of showing programs with a liberal bias that come from the Public Broadcasting Service. (Except for the financial reasons, rejections of network productions by PBS local affiliates are based on the same considerations as those of local commercial stations.)

Fifth, the rejection may be based on personal or political considerations. A station owner, manager, or board of directors might not want the public to get information that may expose or embarrass a favored person or institution or jeopardize a particular cause.

Regardless of the reason, local news consumers should be aware that they have little or no way of finding out whether they were deprived of information or points of view available to most other people in the country. They should also consider how the affiliate power to reject a certain program (and thus decrease network advertising income for that program) might influence what the networks decide to produce in the first place. Will the threat of affiliate rejection force the networks to be more responsible, more courageous—or more timid?

MEDIA DECISIONS

1. On 6 June 1973, "literally thousands" of irate viewers clogged the thirteen incoming telephone lines of CBS affiliate WCCO-TV, in Minneapolis–Saint Paul, to complain about that station's decision to cut live coverage of the Senate hearings on campaign practices (the "Watergate affair"). After carrying the morning's session, the station dropped the hearings and instead plugged in a Minnesota Twins baseball game. Since the networks were rotating coverage of the hearings, and it was CBS's turn for that day, the cutoff denied everyone in the Minneapolis–Saint Paul area the opportunity to view the afternoon testimony at the hearings. According to the station, the public outcry was many times the intensity of that voiced earlier by soap opera fans who were upset when their soap operas were preempted to cover the same Senate hearings.[3]

2. CBS News president Richard Salant, in discussing the effects of Vice-President Agnew's attack on network news analyses immediately following presidential speeches, stated: "One station said it was going to black out our analysis following the president's speeches; other less candid [affiliates] would just do it without saying." [4] In June 1973, CBS itself decided to stop this kind of analysis and delay any analysis to the next day.

3. In early 1971, more than forty of ABC's nearly two hundred affiliates refused to carry the ABC evening news with Howard K. Smith and Harry Reasoner. Instead, most of these affiliates offered movies, reruns, and run-of-the-mill syndicated entertainment shows. At a meeting of ABC affiliate owners, Harry Reasoner severely criticized the affiliates, calling the rejections a "disgrace." This, along with the increased popularity of the news program, caused many of these affiliates to change their mind within a year and carry the program. [5]

4. The Public Broadcasting Service's "Black Journal," as late as 1972 the only regularly scheduled television show written, produced, and directed by blacks, was at one time being rejected by eight public television stations in Alabama alone. The Federal Communications Commission upheld the right of local stations to reject the program. [6] Eleven years earlier, "Walk in My Shoes," a documentary depicting what it was like to be black in the United States, was rejected by more than ten ABC affiliates in the southern states. Some of these affiliates claimed the documentary was too one-sided or might cause racial unrest. [7]

5. In 1968, only 54 of 165 public television stations allowed the showing of a documentary sympathetic to Cuba's Fidel Castro. [8] Some stations also refused to show two programs on China produced by the Canadian Broadcasting Corporation. [9] These stations felt

the programs were biased to favor the Communist governments in the two countries.

"Who Invited Us?", a 1969 National Educational Television historical documentary that focused on a half century of U.S. military intervention abroad, was refused by PBS affiliates in Washington, D.C.; Norfolk and Richmond, Virginia; Austin, Texas; Redding, California; and many other cities.[10]

In October 1972, PBS affiliates in Arkansas, Washington, and Mississippi refused to televise "V.D. Blues," a program designed to educate the public about venereal disease.[11]

ACTIVITIES

1. If possible, interview the manager of a local network affiliate to find out how many programs he has rejected in the last six months and his reasons for doing so.

2. Imagine you are the station manager of a local network affiliate that frequently rejects nationally scheduled network productions.

Write a two- to three-minute speech for broadcast over your station explaining to your audience why you refuse to carry some programs.

3. Imagine that you have just discovered, by reading a magazine article or the television listings from an out-of-town newspaper, that your local NBC affiliate did not carry a reportedly excellent program that you would have loved to see.

Write a letter of complaint to the station management expressing your displeasure and disagreement over their decision not to carry the program.

4. The manager of a local affiliate station has told you that the reason he showed an old movie instead of a network public-affairs program is that he gets more advertising money that way.

Write a brief letter trying to convince him that his obligation to show network public-affairs programs is more important than the increased profits and audience he gets by showing the movie.

QUESTIONS FOR DISCUSSION

1. Should a local station have the right to refuse to carry a nationally scheduled network program for financial, practical, or ideological reasons? Why? Should there be a law forbidding the practice?

2. If a station does refuse to carry a nationally scheduled program, should it inform the audience that it is refusing to do so? Why?

3. Why is it that executives seldom admit rejecting a program because of its political message, but instead state financial, practical, or professional reasons? Which will the public accept as most reasonable?

11

Censorship of Columnists

TEST CASE

The year: 1960. You are the editor of a daily newspaper that regularly carries the syndicated Drew Pearson
column. One of his columns alleges that Vice-President
Richard Nixon's brother, Donald Nixon, secured a loan
of $205,000 on his home—which was valued at less
than $60,000. The loan was from Howard Hughes. The
loan was never repaid, so the house became the property
of the Hughes Tool Company. Noting that a Justice
Department antitrust suit against the Hughes Tool Company was subsequently dropped, Pearson raised the question of a possible conflict of interest between Richard
Nixon's family's financial interests and the government's
case against the tool company. Pearson felt that the case
should be investigated to discover if Nixon or anyone in
the Executive Department had exerted any pressure to
have the Justice Department drop the suit. You are hesi-
tant about running the column until the serious charge
is completely substantiated. However, other papers will
be running the story.

Will you run this column or substitute another in its
place?

**Compare your decision with the one that newspapers
actually made in this situation.**

Of the forty-three New England daily newspapers that
normally ran Pearson's syndicated column, forty chose to
censor it that day. Pearson's follow-up column, which

alleged that the Nixons tried to keep the loan a secret in order to avoid paying taxes on the profit from the sale of the house to the tool company for the price of the loan, was censored by forty-two of the forty-three papers. As of 1973, Pearson's account of the loan still stands as correct.[1]

Just because a newspaper subscribes to the column of a nationally syndicated writer, it is not required to print each column written. When a paper does refuse a column there is usually no official reason given. If asked, the editor will most likely explain that he found the particular column was libelous, had unsubstantiated accusations, or was in bad taste. As one editor put it, he would use any column "as long as it's not libelous, as long as it's germane, or as long as it's not ridiculous or makes the newspaper look ridiculous." The problem is that what is libelous, irrelevant, or ridiculous to one writer, editor, or reader may not be to another.

Unless the reader sees another newspaper that carries the same writer, he or she will have no idea the columnist has been censored for that day. Instead of a blank space, an older column by the same writer or another article will be substituted. Syndicated cartoonists are sometimes treated in the same way.

In addition to nationally syndicated columnists, most newspapers also carry local columnists who write only for that newspaper. Their columns can also be rejected by an editor.

MEDIA DECISIONS

1. In late 1972, the *Providence Journal*, without an official explanation, dropped the regular column of staff writer Hamilton Davis. His liberal column was often critical of Rhode Island politicians. In a protest

to the management, 115 persons in the news operation signed a petition stating:

> It appears that killing the Davis column is only the latest in a series of policy moves that have reduced the flow of ideas in our newspapers. We understand that there are standing orders not to use certain columnists—Wicker, TRB, Von Hoffman, and others. These men do not speak for all of us. But they do offer opinions now unavailable to our readers. . . .[2]

2. Edward Sorel's cartoons were syndicated in the late 1960s by King Features and carried in forty-four daily papers at one time. But they were so controversial that some papers refused to use all that were made available, and more than half of the subscribing papers canceled their subscriptions after a short time. King Features felt that Sorel's work "was of a consistently high quality but perhaps ahead of its time."

Sorel stated:

> It wasn't so much that my ideas were radical as it was that I attacked *everyone*, Richard Nixon, Hubert Humphrey, Timothy Leary, Eldridge Cleaver, Ayn Rand. . . . Compared to the political cartoons of the eighteenth and nineteenth century what I did was very tame, but in the last fifty years the public has become unaccustomed to hard-hitting cartoons.[3]

Garry Trudeau, another cartoonist, had many episodes of his "Doonesbury" comic strip—especially those dealing with the Watergate affair—rejected by the *Washington Post, Boston Globe*, and *Los Angeles Times*, among others. In the editors' viewpoint, these episodes were "prejudicial," "too political," or "offensive to the public."

3. The *St. Petersburg Times* refused to publish a 1971 Jack Anderson column detailing sexual allegations

against nationally syndicated cartoonist Al Capp. Several readers called to complain because they saw the column in another paper. As a result, the paper later published it. In answer to a *Times* questionnaire on the matter, readers voted by a two-to-one margin that they were against the newspaper's initial editorial decision to censor the column.[4]

4. The *New Republic* Feature Syndicate offered Ralph Nader's column, "In the Public Interest," to newspapers. However, it also offered exclusive territorial rights to the column. This guaranteed that, if the newspaper buying the column so requested, no other paper in the area could buy or use the column.

On 29 February 1972, the Riverside, California, *Press-Enterprise* accepted the column and planned to use it immediately. But on March 8, the syndicate wrote back to the executive editor of that paper saying: "The *Los Angeles Times* has decided to take the Nader column. They have asked for exclusive territorial rights and I regret that we can no longer offer the column to you as a result." Although the *Times,* located sixty miles away, now had rights to the column, it never printed it. Nonetheless, it prevented the Riverside paper from using it.

When the *Times* relinquished its rights four months later, the column was again offered to the *Press-Enterprise* who, this time, didn't reply. The result of this episode was that newspaper readers in southern California were not exposed to Ralph Nader's column.[5]

5. Lu Palmer, black columnist for the *Chicago Daily News,* wrote a column in 1973 supporting the efforts of the Black Panthers and other community-based organizations to make policemen accountable for their actions in the black community. The column was rejected because top editors felt that the article would not be believable to the white readers. An editor told Palmer: "We have to protect your credibility with those 90 percent white readers." Responding to Palmer's claim that this was censorship, the editor

replied, "I didn't censor it, I edited it." Palmer replied, "Well, you edited it out." To this, the editor stated, "Well, Lu, I hope you are not questioning my motives."

This was one of two conflicts with top editors that caused Palmer to resign and to state:

> The white establishment press and the honest views of a black journalist are totally incompatible. . . . A viewpoint such as mine will not be respected by the editorial hierarchy and will never be permitted full expression without both overt and covert restraints. . . . Black people have got to establish some alternative forms of communication; we can't deal with this traditional established communication system.[6]

ACTIVITIES

1. Select six columns from the same or different columnists who write for your school or daily newspaper. Select the article that is the most critical of or damaging to powerful people, politicians, or institutions.

Imagine you represent the institution or are the person attacked in the column, and you have found out ahead of time that it is scheduled to be published in a few days. Write a letter to the editor asking him to censor it, pointing out how the article is in bad taste, irresponsible, inaccurate, misleading, inconsistent, or libelous. (Libel is any false statement that purposely attempts to damage a person.)

Exchange the above letter with another student's, along with the column in question, and this time imagine you are a publisher. Respond to the letter by explaining why you will or will not censor the column.

2. Locate three different daily newspapers at your school or community library. Go through five consecutive days for each paper and list all the columnists and cartoonists that are used by each paper.

Imagine you are the editor of a daily newspaper and select from the list the columnists and cartoonists that you would use in your own newspaper. Select only two-thirds of the names.

Did you select these people because of the quality of their work, because you agreed with them, or because you want all representative viewpoints presented in your newspaper?

3. Select a cartoon on the editorial page of your daily newspaper and answer the following questions:

   a. Who are the characters (or who is the character) depicted in the cartoon? If the characters are not meant to be famous people, what group are they supposed to represent (students, the public, Congress, demonstrators, etc.)? What is it that enables you to make the identification (a beard, clothes, signs, etc.)?

   b. What problem, controversy, event, or situation is dealt with, hinted at, mentioned, or pictured in the cartoon?

   c. Does the cartoonist show the characters to be honest, courageous, likable, or respectable, or does he depict them as dishonest, cowardly, confused, stupid, or silly?

   d. What technique is used by the cartoonist? For example, how does he make the character look confused?

   e. If the cartoonist were to write an editorial, what would he say about the situation and the character that he has drawn?

   f. State the facts and reasons in support of your own agreement or disagreement with how you think the cartoonist feels. If you don't have any reasons or facts to back up your position, then why do you feel this way?

   g. Draw your own cartoon of a person or group in your school and try to have the cartoon depict what these people really are, as you see the truth. Use whatever artistic style and exaggeration you need in order to bring out the personality, characteristics, or situations that you want the reader to become aware of.

QUESTIONS FOR DISCUSSION

1. Under what, if any, condition is a newspaper justified in substituting an old column for one scheduled for a particular day?

2. Should the newspaper be required to leave a blank space or include a printed notice to indicate that the column has been censored? Why?

3. Do you think, for example, it is significant that no one in Los Angeles is able to read a columnist on a particular day because of the editor's refusal to run the column, while in San Francisco people can read it? Is being able to censor a columnist a kind of power? Just how great a power is it compared to political or financial power?

12

Censorship of Entertainment

TEST CASE

The year: 1973. You are the president of a television network. "Sticks and Bones," a filmed version of an award-winning stage drama that deals with the callous reception of a Vietnam veteran returning blind from the war, is scheduled to be aired March 9. You have allowed your affiliate stations to see a closed-circuit preview showing of the drama. Sixty-nine out of 184 affiliates have already decided not to carry it because they are concerned about the program and the timing of its presentation. It is scheduled to be shown during the middle of the period when your network is giving feature coverage to the return of POWs from North Vietnam. You think the filmed drama is an excellent production and might even earn an Emmy Award, but you also feel it might offend millions of Americans whose emotions are focused on the returning POWs.

Will you go ahead with your plans to air the program?

Compare your decision with the one that a network president actually made in this situation.

Four days before the set date, CBS-TV president Robert Wood and CBS chairman William S. Paley postponed the airing of the program. In a telegram to all affiliates, Wood explained:

> *In light of recent developments, many of us both at the network and among the stations are now con-*

vinced that . . . presentation on the air of "Sticks and Bones" at this time might be unnecessarily abrasive to the feelings of millions of Americans whose lives or attention are at the moment emotionally dominated by the returning POWs and other veterans who have suffered the ravages of war.

In a statement about affiliates, Wood said that never before had CBS witnessed a "greater or more serious and responsible sense of concern expressed by affiliates about a program and the timing of its broadcast." Another CBS spokesman said that the film would be aired "when the context of its showing will be less distressing and its possible application to actual events less immediate." The producer of the film, Joseph Papp, called the postponement

a cowardly cop-out, a rotten affront to freedom of speech. . . . It is frightening that this monster corporation, CBS, had decided to put its tail between its legs and back away from this program because some affiliates find it too strong stuff. . . . They are accepting control by their affiliates, denying millions the right to see an important work of art. . . . Who is Wood, who is CBS, to decide the mood of the country? [1]

When the drama was finally shown five months later only 91 affiliate stations carried it compared to the 184 that normally carry the network's Friday night programs. Advertisers also shied away by withdrawing their commercials from the program.

Bias that is the hardest to detect or explain is the most effective bias in the long run; people absorb it unknowingly. When a person claims to be objective and then displays obvious bias, he is often ineffective and may even produce the opposite reaction and attitude from what he desires. Obvious bias puts readers or listeners on guard and makes them question the credibility of the news agency involved.

People tend to forget about political bias when it comes in the form of entertainment. Thus entertainment serves as the perfect and most effective carrier of bias. At the same time they are enjoying the entertainment, people unknowingly absorb the political, social, and economic messages that are assumed in the program.

In the form of a dramatic story, comic strip, cartoon, comedy, or variety show, a message gets across to the viewer with much more impact and validity than it would in a newscast. In addition, our total consumption of entertainment outweighs that of news and public affairs manyfold. As children, during the most impressionable years of our lives, we consume entertainment almost exclusively. By the time the average child is five years old he will have spent more time watching television than he will later spend in the college classroom.

There is a strong political, social, and economic bias in the mere depiction of a certain life-style as desirable, glamorous, or prestigious. The favorable depiction of a life-style of material acquisition and consumption tends to create support for policies favoring production and profit whether or not the producer designed the program with this support in mind. The favorable depiction of a life-style of environmental concern and service to others tends to support policies favoring conservation and social services.

Being a powerful instrument of persuasion, entertainment has always been subject to censorship. In the 1950s, censorship of television and radio by sponsors and advertising agencies—with the cooperation of the networks and stations—affected every program. Today, censorship of entertainment is not so widespread as in past decades, but it still exists.

Citizens should be just as concerned and aware of censorship in entertainment as they are about censorship of the news. They should be aware of the different kinds of censorship: censorship of political and economic ideas, censorship of obscenity and profanity, or censorship of the favorable depiction of crime and violence. Further, citizens should be able to distinguish between the different methods of censorship available to broadcasters: banning a complete program, editing out parts, or scheduling a program at an unlikely hour.

MEDIA DECISIONS

1. Interviewed on NBC's "Today" show, comedian George Jessel made disparaging remarks about the *New York Times* and the *Washington Post*, referring to them as *"Pravda"* (the large Russian newspaper that prints the official line of the Communist government). Edwin Newman, the interviewer, objected to Jessel's statement.

Jessel responded, "You have your opinions and I have mine."

With one minute left in the interview, Jessel said, "I just wanted to say one more thing."

Newman said, "Please don't," and then cut short the interview.

NBC News president Reuven Frank supported Newman's action, saying, "He acted wisely and in the best possible taste to correct a live broadcast situation which seemed to be getting out of hand." [2]

2. In the late 1960s the Smothers brothers had a weekly entertainment-comedy program that often poked fun at or criticized people and policies. According to the brothers, 75 percent of their programs had sections edited out by CBS network management before being sent to the affiliate stations. Many affiliate stations then censored the tapes on their own or blipped out pieces as the show came over the air. [3] Finally, CBS canceled the show, claiming that the brothers failed to cooperate with CBS previewing

policies. The brothers took the network to court for the cancellation and, in 1973, won a $776,000 settlement. A CBS countersuit, contending that the brothers broke the contract by not cooperating with previewing policies, was rejected by the same U.S. District Court jury.

On one "Smothers Brothers" show in 1967, Pete Seeger, the famous radical folk singer who was blacklisted by broadcasters for seventeen years, was asked by CBS to drop the following verse from one of his songs. It referred to the position in which the United States found itself in Vietnam:

> But every time I read the papers
> That old feeling comes on;
> We're waist deep in the Big Muddy
> And the big fool says to push on. ©

When Seeger refused to drop the verse, CBS censored the entire song. Seeger commented, "It is wrong for anyone to censor what I consider my most important statement to date. . . . I think the public should know that the airwaves are censored for ideas as well as for sex." [4]

3. For many years both mass media executives and the advertising agencies that produced programs banned hundreds of liberal and radically oriented entertainers from appearing on television. Perhaps the most famous was a black man, Paul Robeson. Robeson was an all-American football player, linguist, world-renowned actor, concert and popular singer. A democratic socialist, he crusaded for the rights of black and poor people the world over. Many accused him of being a Communist.[5] One of the reasons the ban against Robeson was so complete was that blacks owned no television stations in the 1950s and 1960s.

4. Fifteen minutes into an ABC special rock concert in November 1972, the president of Taft Broadcasting, Lawrence H. Rogers II, found the Alice Cooper rock

group so offensive that he ordered his Cincinnati station to yank it off the air. Carloads of young people began picketing station WKRC and, in the next few days, four thousand letters were received. Four out of five letters denounced Rogers's decision. The station then announced it would telecast an edited version of the show at a later date.

Another station, WPVI-TV in Philadelphia, attempted to prevent children from watching the rock concert by delaying it from 10:30 P.M to 1:30 A.M.[6]

5. In 1964, NBC refused to show MGM-produced "Dr. Kildare" and "Mr. Novak" dramas dealing with venereal disease because they touched on sexual intimacies which the network felt were not appropriate for the audience. MGM producers were greatly angered, and the surgeon general of the United States pleaded with NBC to reconsider. He pointed out that venereal disease had been increasing at a shocking rate, especially among teen-agers, and that stories related to veneral disease on programs with such large teen-age audiences would greatly benefit the government in warning citizens of the growing problem. The network denied the request.[7]

ACTIVITIES

1. List the topics or kinds of information that seem to be censored the most. Other than the cases mentioned above, list the censor, the subject matter, and the method involved in cases of censorship that you know or have read about.

2. Does your school restrict the kind of music played over the public-address system at noontime or by the school band at a half-time football show? Does the school restrict or forbid criticism of school practices, teachers, or administrators in the entertainment sections of the school paper or in assemblies? Describe the restrictions. If the school doesn't describe the re-

strictions officially in writing, find out what individual makes the final decision regarding what is acceptable. Describe his or her ideas of what is appropriate at school activities or in the paper.

3. Define obscenity according to your own standards. Briefly compare your definition with how your community, school, and courts have defined obscenity.

QUESTIONS FOR DISCUSSION

1. Does watching a critical, obscene, or violent film or performance cause some people to act in a disrespectful, illegal, obscene, or violent manner? Or for most people does it merely serve as an emotional release and thus decrease the tendency to actually commit such acts?

2. By allowing a certain amount of severe criticism of authority, or a certain amount of obscenity, does a country weaken its moral fiber? If so, should free speech be limited in order to maintain society's moral and ethical standards? Should the same limitations apply to schools, radio, television, movies, stage plays, newspapers, and books? If not, how should the standards differ?

3. Under what conditions, if any, is censorship of political and economic ideas in entertainment justified? Can the mass media's widespread censorship of such ideas restrict the alternative viewpoints that most of the public will consider? If so, will this strengthen or weaken our democracy?

13

Censorship of Advertising

TEST CASE

The year: 1972. You are the president of one of the three national TV networks. The Allstate Insurance Company wants to pay for commercials showing that air bags are an effective and foolproof device for protecting passengers. The commercials show how the air bags performed in a series of road tests. This is an important issue which may affect federal auto-safety legislation. Some of your largest advertisers (auto manufacturers), who disagree with Allstate, probably won't be pleased to see such commercials and might even ask for free time to show an ad outlining their own positions.

Will you allow Allstate to show the commercials?

Compare your decision with the one the networks actually made in this situation.

All three networks refused to let Allstate run any of the commercials. The vice-president of the insurance company stated: "[because] some automobile manufacturers object to safety devices, I don't think Allstate should have been denied access to the airwaves." He commented that he didn't know whether auto manufacturers had put pressure on the networks to refuse commercials: "I am not alleging that any pressure was put on the networks. All I know is that they are the only public opponents of air bags that I know of." [1]

Most people would agree that media owners have a right to refuse ads that are fraudulent, misleading, or in bad taste. But do owners also have a right to censor some political ads and to permit others? Some stations and newspapers answer no. Their policy is to accept advertising on controversial issues from all viewpoints. Other newspapers (approximately 50 percent as revealed in a recent survey) say yes.[2] They believe it is management's prerogative to censor ads with controversial messages that, in their eyes, are in bad taste, against the public interest, or too controversial.

Does such censorship in effect deny free speech to some advertisers and deprive the people of important political viewpoints? If so, is the censorship of advertising with controversial political, social, or economic messages a matter of public concern?

MEDIA DECISIONS

1. An organization of business executives requested advertising time in 1971 to present their case against the Nixon administration's policy in Vietnam. Many stations refused. The FCC upheld the stations' right to refuse to sell time. However, a U.S. court of appeals overruled the FCC and held that a station cannot refuse to sell commercial time to an individual or group just because the station has a policy of not selling time for controversial views or because it fears it would have to provide free rebuttal time under the Fairness Doctrine.[3]

In May 1973, the Supreme Court overturned the court of appeals by ruling that neither the Constitution nor federal communications law requires stations to sell commercial air time for statements on matters of public controversy. Chief Justice Warren E. Burger, delivering the majority opinion, held that stations have been given "journalistic discretion" to deny access to individuals and groups who wish to pay for and present their own editorial advertisements. He also noted that forcing stations to sell time to organizations that can afford to buy it could give an unfair advantage to those with money. In dissent, Justices William Brennan and Thurgood Marshall said that the majority ruling violates traditional free-speech priorities by giving more access right to persons with a commercial message than to those with a political message and that the public has a legitimate interest "in receiving ideas and information directly from the advocates of those ideas, without the interposition of journalistic middlemen."

2. A candidate for the U.S. Senate from Georgia, J. B. Stoner, ran ads on two television stations, stating: "I am the only candidate for U.S. senator who is for white people. I am the only candidate who is against integration. . . . The main reason why niggers want integration is because niggers want our white women."

The Atlanta National Association for the Advancement of Colored People (NAACP) requested that the Federal Commmunications Commisssion ban the ads because they could incite violence. The FCC ruled that no exceptions should be made to broadcast regulations that make it illegal to censor political ads. The commission stated that only a clear and present danger of imminent violence might warrant interference with a political commercial. The commission added that if there is to be free speech it must be for things we abhor and hate as well as for things we agree with.[4]

3. For over a month, the *New York Times* refused to run an advertisement alleging that *Times* associate editor and columnist Tom Wicker was guilty of a list of errors in the columns favoring the Democratic Presidential candidate, Senator George McGovern, and criticizing President Nixon's statements on Vietnam. The *Times* insisted the ad must first be checked out for accuracy with Wicker, who was on vacation. The group detailing the errors, Accuracy in the Media (AIM), felt this amounted to censorship of the right to say what it wanted, when it wanted, in a way it

wanted, and that furthermore, it could document all the statements in the ad. A few weeks later, in August 1972, AIM had no trouble in publishing the ad in the *Washington Star-News* under the heading CENSORED BY THE *NEW YORK TIMES*.[5]

4. During the Vietnam war, *San Francisco Examiner* publisher Charles Gould accepted advertisements for antiwar demonstrations even though he opposed the demonstrations editorially. He felt the ads were bad for the country, but, as he stated it, "not to let them into the paper would be worse for the country." [6]

5. In 1969, the Amalgamated Clothing Workers of America wanted to buy space for a full-page ad in all four Chicago dailies. The ad explained why people should buy American-made men's wear instead of foreign imports. The ad identified Marshall Field and Company department store as the largest importer of foreign clothing. That department store is also one of the largest regular advertisers in Chicago newspapers. All four papers rejected the ad.

The union took the case to court, claiming: "There is no satisfactory substitute for one who is denied access to newspaper space for the expression of idea or opinion." The union claimed that since newspapers are semipublic entities that affect the public interest, they should be obligated by law to permit all persons to purchase space for the expression of ideas or opinions.

A federal district court rejected the union's argument and ruled: "Political advertisements are constitutionally protected to no greater or lesser extent than other forms of speech, and interference by state actions with such expression is prohibited." The U.S. Supreme Court let the ruling stand.[7]

ACTIVITIES

1. In weekly papers or magazines, find three advertisements that you think your school or daily paper or

local television station would reject either because the ads are in bad taste, might be obscene, or are too strong a political or social statement.

Explain why you think the ads would be censored.

2. Should your school newspaper print every advertisement it receives? Why? Briefly describe the type of advertisements, if any, that you think your school paper should reject.

3. Write one advertisement with a political or social message that would probably have trouble being accepted by a conservative media agency because it is too radical. Then write one that has such a far-right message that a liberal media agency might not accept it.

QUESTIONS FOR DISCUSSION

1. Does the public generally have any way of knowing that an advertisement has been rejected? Is the agency that rejected the ad likely to draw attention to the fact? Why?

2. Should ads with serious political or social messages from all political viewpoints be accepted equally, or should ads expressing the so-called extreme political views be censored?

3. If it is legal to manufacture and sell a product such as cigarettes, why should the government or news agencies have a right to forbid the advertisement of such?

14

Censorship of Organizations and Groups

The year: 1972. You are the president of a national TV network. The American Security Council wants to buy time on your network to show "Only the Strong." This documentary explains why the United States should not enter into any arms-limitation agreement with Russia and why it should instead increase defense spending in order to retain military superiority. The film takes a strong stand on these controversial issues and you feel sure that groups with opposing messages will request free air time to present their side. In addition, you feel your news department has done a good job of presenting both sides of this issue and that the balance you have achieved would be upset by the presentation of this documentary.

Will you sell the American Security Council air time so it can present its documentary to the people?

Compare your decision with the one that the networks actually made in this situation.

All three networks refused to sell time to the group. However, more than two hundred individual stations showed the film; some of them did so free as a public service.[1]

Many groups of citizens and even congressmen feel at times that radio and television news and public-affairs programming is either not presenting their views to the public or is doing so in an unfair manner. To compensate, some people or groups try to communicate directly over television or radio. But two things often prevent their gaining access. The price is one: it takes between $90,000 and $150,000 to buy a half hour of network prime time. Ten minutes of network radio time costs about $4,000. In addition, to produce a good program or half-hour documentary can cost up to $250,000. Second, even if the group or person has enough money, the networks may refuse to allow them to broadcast their presentation.

The networks may explain their refusal by noting that the program does not meet their journalistic standards or might upset the balance they are maintaining by their own fair coverage of the issue. If they air a program that upsets the balance, they could be forced to give opposing groups free time. Another reason given by one network was that selling time to individuals or groups gives an unfair advantage to those with money—a surprising explanation since the networks have always allowed the large corporations to buy an unlimited amount of television time to show commercials in support of their own positions on such isssues as the need for the Alaska pipeline, more electric or atomic power, strip mining, and insecticides. Lastly, the networks or stations may refuse to sell time because they don't want to upset the regular program schedule.

MEDIA DECISIONS

1. In 1969, "Citizens Against ABM [antiballistic missile system]," a nonpartisan group of scientists, politicians, and celebrities, offered to purchase a half hour of television time to present their case against increased defense spending. All three networks refused.[2]

2. The national citizens' lobby Common Cause attempted to buy time in 1971 to present its case against the administration's policy in Vietnam. All three networks refused, claiming that this would upset their balance on the issue and give an advantage to those with money. Common Cause finally did manage to purchase time from sixty-five independent stations.[3]

3. In May 1972, the three networks refused to sell time to a group of fourteen U.S. senators and representatives who wanted to reply to President Nixon's broadcast announcing the mining of North Vietnam's waters.[4] The FCC supported the networks' refusal by ruling that legislators have no right to buy network time to make their views known.

4. Political candidates appeared on WSAZ-TV in Huntington, West Virginia, and WPKE in Pikeville, Kentucky, in 1967, and branded as Communists all who opposed strip mining. Two community organizers asked to buy time on these stations in order to answer the candidates' charges, but the request was rejected. The Federal Communications Commission decided in favor of the community organizers, but, by that time, the election was over.[5]

5. Former Secretary of the Interior Walter J. Hickel arranged with the NBC radio network in 1971 to carry his speech, for which he had found a commercial sponsor, on its 234 affiliated radio stations. The speech argued for a change in priorities in order to protect the environment. After previewing the text of the speech, NBC reversed itself and advised Hickel that they would not sell him air time because the speech was "too controversial" and that stations broadcasting the speech might be required to allow free time to those with opposing points of view. Hickel replied, "If my speech is considered too controversial to be broadcast . . . then I can only ask, 'where is freedom of speech?' " One sentence that NBC cited as too controversial was: "I'll argue until I die that there is not

enough government in areas which are choking the living of life in modern America—areas such as transportation, the environment, and the urban crises." [6]

ACTIVITIES

1. Imagine that you are the president of a television network and that you have just previewed what you judge to be an unfair documentary attempting to prove that the United States should not trade with Communist or socialist nations. The citizens' group that produced it has asked to buy time on your network in order to show this documentary to the American people. Write as many reasons as you can think of for refusing. Or, explain why you would sell time to the group.

2. Imagine you are the president of an environmental group that wishes to convince the public that pollution of the oceans endangers man's survival. A television network claims your documentary is journalistically unsound and unbalanced. Write a letter to the network protesting their refusal to sell your organization a half hour of television time for the purpose of showing your organization's film.

3. Briefly describe what kind of a controversial show you would like to present over network television if you had the $150,000 necessary to purchase a half hour of prime time.

QUESTIONS FOR DISCUSSION

1. Should proponents of one side of an argument, who have lots of money, be allowed to buy program time or numerous advertisements to support their position even though supporters of other positions are shut out completely just because they have no money? Is

this free speech? What can be done to equalize such a situation in broadcasting and in the print media?

2. Is there considerable power in being able to determine whether a group shall be able to buy television time to communicate to the American people? Is it greater or less power than that of a corporation or union president, a congressman, a senator, or a president? Why?

Books for Further Study

Cirino, Robert. *Don't Blame the People: How the News Media Use Bias, Distortion and Censorship to Manipulate Public Opinion.* New York: Vintage Books, 1972. From a very liberal viewpoint.

Keeley, Joseph. *The Left-Leaning Antenna: A Political Bias in Television.* New Rochelle, N.Y.: Arlington House, 1971. A study of bias in television news and entertainment—from a very conservative viewpoint.

McClellan, Grant. *Censorship in the U.S.A.* New York: H. W. Wilson, 1967.

Wise, David. *The Politics of Lying.* New York: Random House, 1973. An examination of cases where the government attempted to deceive the public.

III

IN THE ADVERTISERS' INTEREST

It is very costly to set up and operate a broadcasting system. Thus the question naturally arises of the best way to finance the system and at the same time best serve the people and country. Outside the U.S., most systems depend on public and government support. Canada spends $6.00 per person per year on noncommercial public television; England, $3.29 per person; and Japan, $2.90. Other democracies such as Israel, Germany, Italy, Holland, Belgium, Austria, Denmark, and Sweden spend as much or more. Such moneys come from the people in the form of taxes and/or license fees imposed on owners of television sets. These license fees range from around $6.00 to $40.00 a year depending on the country.

Canada, England, and Japan permit commercial broadcasting for profit on a very limited basis, and, as a result, it comes in second in the competition for audiences. The other group of nations mentioned above forbids commercial broadcasting entirely; some of the countries accept advertising on the public stations in order to help pay costs, but none allow commercials to determine or interrupt programs. Each of these public systems has devised a management structure that insures a large degree of financial and editorial independence from the government that created them.

In sharp contrast, the United States spends only $.80 per person per year on noncommercial public broadcasting. With such low funding, it can't hope to compete with a commercial broadcasting system that spends $13.71 per person. This money comes from advertisers instead of from the people. It makes quite a difference in the technical and artistic quality of a program as well as in the amount of advance publicity a program will receive. On an average evening, over 95 per cent of the television audience will watch commercial broadcasting while less than 5 percent will watch public television.[1]

Programming by commercial broadcasting reflects this dependence on advertising. Although broadcasters in the democracies listed above allocate a good portion of prime time television for public affairs, the U.S. networks average about 2 percent. Such programming attracts smaller audiences than are attracted by entertainment programming. The major effort, money, talent, and technology are spent trying to devise an overall program schedule that will attract the largest audiences and thus bring in the most advertising money. Cultural and public-affairs programming and the public interest often take second place.

There is fierce competition among the different commercial networks and stations. But it is competition among similar types of programming for the advertising dollar, not the competition of different programming representing various viewpoints or tastes. True, the networks do provide some news or live coverage that results in financial loss, but such programs are considered necessary to maintain credibility and prestige. Programming resulting from dependence on advertising has an inherent bias apart from its content or style of presentation. It is hard for many people to believe that the country really faces serious crises when there is so much time spent on entertainment and so little on public affairs. In addition, investigative journalism and more serious entertainment programs may not be shown if it is feared they will bring about a loss of advertising.

Of course, there are courageous advertisers who

have sponsored documentaries that appeal to smaller audiences. In the early 1960s, Bell and Howell continued to sponsor controversial documentaries even though some school superintendents and dealers notified the company they would no longer use Bell and Howell equipment because of their sponsorship.[2] The company responded by stating that public-affairs programs should be free of advertiser influence or censorship of any kind.

Bell and Howell was the exception. As a rule, advertisers want to sponsor programs that serve their own interest. As late as 1961, Procter and Gamble, the largest television advertiser, had a written program-buying policy that directed how $100,000,000 of advertising should be used to influence content:

> There will be no material on any of our programs which could in any way further the concept of business as cold, ruthless, and lacking all sentiment or spiritual motivation. . . . There will be no material that may give offense either directly or by inference to any organized minority group, lodge or other organizations, institutions, residents of any states or sections of the country, or a commercial organization of any sort.[3]

Such written policies are no longer used, but the unwritten policy of advertisers to shy away from controversial or serious programs still exists.

Advertisers claim they are sponsoring what the majority of people want as proven by the popularity of programs, and that therefore they are serving the public. Critics respond by saying the majority have been conditioned to want watered-down programs because they have not been offered any real alternatives since the day they first watched television or listened to the radio. Critics also contend that the type of programming that the majority like and that advertisers will pay for is not necessarily in the public interest, and they note further that since all networks and stations aim for the broadest possible audience in order to increase advertising, there is little or no programming for minority groups or those with special interests and tastes.

Unlike commercial broadcasting, newspapers and mass-circulation magazines are supported to some degree directly by the people in the form of a news-stand purchase price or subscription. On the average, however, this money covers only 30 percent of the production costs of daily newspapers and mass-circulation magazines. In other words, the reader pays $.15 for a newspaper that cost $.50 to produce; the other $.35, plus the profit margin, is paid for by the advertisers.

If a publication cannot attract advertisers it may fail no matter how many millions of people buy it or how great its journalists are. Both *Look* and *Life* failed despite their large circulations (over seven million each). A major reason was their failure to attract enough advertisers who could pay as much as $65,000 for a full-page ad. Some publications get along on subscriptions and sales alone, but they can't hope to become mass-circulation magazines unless they can attract the big advertising money. This being the case, the editors of mass-circulation publications, like broadcasters, have to design a product primarily for the purposes of attracting advertising and for attracting the type of readership that can be sold to advertisers. All too often, journalistic considerations come second.

15

Programming

TEST CASE

The year: 1970. You are the president of one of the big three TV networks. Your first obligation is to make decisions that increase profits for your stockholders. Although news anthologies and documentaries bring in less advertising money than entertainment shows, you would like to have at least some prime time (7:30 P.M. to 11:00 P.M.) regularly set aside for such programming because you feel it is in the public interest to do so.

Out of twenty-one hours per week of prime time programming, you are presently devoting one hour a month to news anthologies and documentaries and the rest of the time to the more profitable entertainment programs such as films, Westerns, family drama, adventure, mystery, comedy, music, and sports. There is about a fifty-fifty chance that you can add one more hour per month of news anthologies and documentaries without causing the stockholders to lose money. Will you take the chance?

Compare your decision with similar ones actually made by the networks.

During the 1970–71 season, ABC had no regularly scheduled news anthologies or documentaries in prime time. NBC allotted one half hour per week and CBS allotted one hour per week. For the American public, this meant that during prime time viewing hours they had a choice of watching programs devoted to controversial is-

111

sues only 2 percent of the time. Over 96 percent of the
time they had no choice but to watch entertainment pro-
grams. All three networks increased slightly the amount
of prime time regularly devoted to news anthologies and
documentaries for the 1972–73 season.[1] For 1973–74, CBS
and ABC scheduled one half hour per week; NBC allotted
no time for programs of this type. All three announced
they would have documentary specials, but not on a
regularly scheduled basis.

Can anybody possibly know what television program everybody in the country is watching at the same
time? No, at least not yet. But the Nielsen rating system tries to make an accurate estimate by placing
monitors on twelve hundred representative families in
order to project what percentage of the national audience is watching a particular show at any given time.
The Nielsen estimates can't be completely accurate;
nevertheless, these ratings are what count in television.
The networks' dependence on the ratings led *Variety's*
critic Les Brown to comment: "Television is not so
interested in the business of communications as it is in
the business of delivering people to advertisers. People
are the merchandise, not the shows. The shows are
merely the bait." [2] Generally, the greater the audience
—as indicated by the Nielsen rating—the more advertising money and profits a network can expect. However, sometimes the type of audience is also taken into
consideration. Audiences such as poor blacks and the
aged, because they have less buying power, are not as
desirable as younger middle-class audiences. As a
result, few programs are designed to attract those with
low buying power.

On the whole, programs that deal seriously and
realistically with life and society attract smaller audiences than the lighter entertainment programs.
Furthermore, it is hard to find an advertiser for serious

programs because sponsors do not want their product associated with such negative elements as injustice, unhappiness, frustration, or conflict—which are often part of a serious treatment of any issue. And if a serious program exposes the wrongdoings of a company that is sponsoring another big show, that company could threaten to take its advertising money to another network.

As a result of these limiting factors, television writers are very much restricted. As Christopher Knopf, television scriptwriter and past president of the Writers Guild, stated, "In documentaries and in news, certain truths can be told, but you can't tell them in commercial drama. You can't take up real problems seriously. . . . We're feeding middle America all the pap we know as lies and nonsense; we are feeding things we personally resent, which have no resemblance to real life." [3]

MEDIA DECISIONS

1. Described as "witty, thoughtful, and attractive" by *Newsweek* magazine, Dick Cavett was told by ABC management that he had three months to improve the Nielsen rating for his late-night talk show or the show would be dropped. This, despite an Emmy Award, praise from ABC management, and critical acclaim. The ratings showed that only five million were watching Cavett compared to thirteen million for Johnny Carson and twelve million for CBS films. Eventually Cavett's program was reduced to one week a month instead of being dropped completely.

2. The "Red Skelton" and "Jackie Gleason" shows were dropped by CBS for the 1970–71 season even though they had very high ratings. But these ratings also showed they were attracting mainly juveniles and people over fifty years of age, groups that are

harder to sell to advertisers. Top management figured
they could produce shows for less money that would
at the same time appeal to younger adults who are
high consumers.[4]

3. In 1970, station WTOP-TV in Washington, D.C.,
complained that advertisers were not supporting its
black-oriented programming because the ratings were
slight for such programs. This, the station stated, was
because black households were not adequately represented in the rating's sample families.[5]

4. Testifying at a January 1973 FCC hearing on
children's television, an NBC attorney frankly admitted that over the past few years his network had
tried to be innovative and imaginative and had lost
money as a result. Beginning with the 1969–70 season,
he said, NBC altered its Saturday morning children's
schedule by taking out unmotivated violence, upgrad-
ing program quality, integrating information with entertainment, and aiming at specific age-groups—things
that are recommended by public-interest groups wanting to reform children's programming. He pointed to
an audience decline of 25 percent since 1968, while
CBS had improved 15 percent and ABC was up 30
percent, and to the fact that NBC had been forced to
slice its advertising prices 10 to 15 percent in 1972.
He also told the FCC commissioners that NBC's voluntary effort to reach narrow age-groups had failed
miserably, and if the government tried to force all
three networks to do the same, it would be depriving
some children of programs that appeal to them. He
concluded by stating that "you can't legislate" good
children's television.[6]

5. Network emphasis on football is understandable;
in a two-week period in January 1973, five of the
eight programs that topped the Nielsen audience
ratings were football games or game previews. The
super bowl, number one, brought in $200,000 per
minute of advertising money. "All in the Family,"

number two in the ratings, brought in $120,000 per minute.

The popularity of a sport alone does not always determine what sporting event will be telecast. Golf receives much more exposure than some more popular sports. Television critic Les Brown surmised that this is probably because golf is the favorite recreational activity of TV executives, ad agency men, and their clients, and further, that golf reaches an affluent audience. Basketball appeals to a larger audience, but in one case, in 1969, the advertising manager of a major company ruled out sponsoring that sport because it appeals to blacks—not an element of the audience that he wanted his product associated with.[7]

ACTIVITIES

1. Imagine you are the program director for a nonprofit television station. Your purpose is not to sell advertising but to program in a way that will entertain, inform, and increase your audience. Briefly outline the types of programs you will put on at prime time hours (7:30 P.M to 11:00 P.M.) during an average week.

2. Make a list of topics that you feel are not dealt with forthrightly or at all in television entertainment. Then interview five adults to see whether they would like to see more or less inclusion of these topics in dramas, comedy, and variety shows. What were their reasons? Finally, of the programs that now appear, find out which they would like to see more of and less of.

3. Make a list of five major advertisers. List topics that each would probably not want to see dealt with in entertainment that they sponsor. For example, a clothing manufacturer will not want to sponsor a drama with a scene showing a child burning because her pajamas caught fire.

QUESTIONS FOR DISCUSSION

1. Given the greater amount of time devoted to entertainment and its freer use of artistic techniques of persuasion, do you feel that in the long run it is as important as newscasts are in influencing public opinion? Why or why not? Give an example of public opinion about an issue and relate it to how that issue has been or is dealt with by television entertainment.

2. Do the vast majority of the public demand the type of programming the networks give them, or are they partly conditioned to want this kind of entertainment by watching commercial broadcasting from an early age? Do you agree with critics who say that the public is addicted to a certain type of programming because for years no real alternative was offered over the mass media?

3. What financial interests do broadcasters have in sports? How are advertising, public enthusiasm for sports, the building of a civic sports stadium, and sports coverage related to each other? What is the relationship between sports and patriotism as you define the word? Could a politician lose favor in the eyes of the media and the people if he opposed the use of public funds for the building of a new stadium? To what extent is the people's response a result of sports programming?

4. Why do professional sports get so much attention compared to amateur sports? Which should get the most sports coverage in the local daily newspaper and stations: little league, high school, college, or professional sports?

16

News Priorities

TEST CASE

You are the news editor of a large daily newspaper and are responsible for establishing news priorities and making up the front page.

Approximately what percentage of your front-page space will you generally allocate to high-interest but trivial stories (beauty contests, movie stars, the weather, photos of animals at the zoo, minor but sensational crimes, accidents) as compared to more serious news?

Compare your decision with the one that newspapers actually made in this situation.

Newspapers vary considerably in the amount of front-page space they allocate to trivial stories; some allocate only 10 percent or less, others allocate over 50 percent. A spot survey of front-page space of America's most respected newspaper reveals a near-total neglect of some very serious problems. For two-month periods in 1950, 1960, and 1969 (a total of six months), the New York Times had a total of 2 articles on population and birth control, 2 on pollution, 1 on hunger in the United States, and none on world hunger. Yet, during these same six months, the paper had 10 front-page articles on the entertainment world, 19 articles with 7 photos on other trivia, 35 articles with 5 photos on religious news, and 44 articles with 19 photos on accidents. For the same periods, the Los Angeles Times had 33 articles with 10

*photos on the entertainment world, 73 articles with 13
photos on other trivia, 25 articles with 2 photos on religious news, and 283 articles with 46 photos on accidents.
On one single day in 1960 the Los Angeles paper had 5
different accident stories on the front page.[1]*

The neglect of important news is not always the
result of deliberate editorial suppression. Many of the
significant trends or events in our world are just not
"newsworthy." Events that happened an hour ago;
events that have a beginning, a climax, and an end;
events that can be photographed or recorded—these
are what make news.

But a news agency can play down sensational happenings and instead feature the significant events and
trends that usually don't make news. To do this, a
station or publication must have its news priorities in
order. News priorities determine what kind of stories
a newspaper will consider important and the amount
of effort and money they will spend on such stories.

As much as anything else, news priorities reveal
the underlying bias of a publication, station, or entire
communications system. Through its news priorities, an
agency communicates to the people the relative importance of things in a very subtle, persuasive, and
repetitive manner that is seldom questioned or taken
into consideration by the news consumer.

The hiring policy of a news agency is one expression of priorities. One daily newspaper may hire
numerous foreign reporters. Another may hire mainly
local reporters. One will hire a labor reporter instead
of a food reporter, or a financial reporter instead of a
science reporter.

Where a station uses its resources is a second expression of news priorities. Two or three reporters and
cameramen might be assigned to cover the airport
arrival of a vice-president and none assigned to cover
important Senate or regulator-agency hearings.

Because both hiring and using reporters and money are behind-the-scene decisions, few news consumers know anything about them. However, by paying attention to the amount of space or time a station or publication gives to certain types of stories, the consumer can tell pretty much what kind of reporters are hired and where money is being spent. If an agency hires no education reporters it isn't likely to have a front page, front cover, or special report on education. If it utilizes no reporters to investigate the causes of local pollution, it isn't likely to give the topic much space or time.

Most stations and publications also have access to regular wire service stories or photos on any number of topics and events. The featuring of certain types of wire service stories (news of trivia or accidents) over others (hard or background news) reveals a station's or publication's ideas of what kind of stories are important and the degree to which it will feature the sensational just to get readers.

Rather than automatically accepting as important the events or trends that are prominently featured, a news consumer should develop his own standard of importance. Then he can determine whether a news agency's priorities are based mostly on political bias, the need to attract additional readers and advertising, or the desire to inform the public about what is really important.

MEDIA DECISIONS

1. The most important single decision made by a magazine's editor is the selection of what issue, event, or person will be featured on the front cover. A survey of the cover stories of *Time, Newsweek, Life,* and *Look* from January 1962 through July 1969 shows that they had a total of 3 cover stories on pollution, 3 on population and birth control, 1 on world hunger, and 2 on the military-industrial complex. There were no

cover stories on such important issues as hunger in the
United States, illiteracy, prison brutality, venereal
disease, chemical-biological warfare, or abortion. In
sharp contrast, during this same seven and a half years,
the four magazines had a total of 35 covers on athletics,
182 on entertainers, 64 on the space program, 40 on
religion, 91 on Vietnam, and 56 on corporations.[2]

2. The "Watergate affair," the discovery and disclosure of illegal acts of political espionage and sabotage against the Democratic party—as planned and
carried out by President Nixon's top advisers and
members of his own committee for reelection—was one
of the major stories of 1972 and 1973. News agencies
differed greatly in the number of full-time reporters
they assigned to investigate the affair in its earlier
stages. From June through the presidential election in
November 1972, the Newhouse newspaper chain,
with 21 Washington reporters, had none on the case.
The Gannett chain, with 12 reporters in Washington,
had none; the Copley chain, with 7, had none; ABC,
with 16, had none; CBS, with 25, had none; NBC, with
25, had one; *Time*, with 19, had one; *Newsweek*, with
26, had one; *U.S. News & World Report*, with 56, had
none; AP, with 65, had none; and UPI, with 51, had
none.

In contrast, the *Washington Post* had 2 full-time
reporters on the story and the *Los Angeles Times*,
with 17 reporters in Washington, assigned 3 to the
story. These two newspapers came up with the most
revelations about the illegal activities during the campaign.[3]

3. A review of three different Chicago television
network affiliates' 10:00 P.M. half-hour newscasts for
a single evening gave an indication of the high priority
given to sports and weather in local newscasts. Out of
news time of 20:17 (NBC), 17:46 (ABC), and 18:50
(CBS) minutes, they spent 6:56, 6:15, and 6:07 minutes
respectively on sports and the weather.[4]

Employment practices also reveal a station's news

priorities. In New York City's six commercial TV stations, there are 8 anchor men, 7 sports reporters, 5 weathermen, 5 entertainment critics, 2 full-time political reporters, 3 full-time science reporters, and 1 full-time investigative reporter.[5]

4. An examination of Philadelphia's three daily newspapers during six days chosen at random in July and August 1971 revealed the following news priorities:

a. The papers devoted 3.5 percent of their space to local news.

b. The three papers gave almost as much space to comics as they did to local news.

c. One paper, the *News,* ran twice as many amusement inches, 25 percent more photographs, and almost as much sports copy as its competitors, even though it is half their size.

d. The *Inquirer* ran six times more women's features than foreign news. The *Bulletin* ran 2.7 times more financial news than national news, and the *News* ran more comics than national news.

e. Advertisers took over 65.5 percent of the *Bulletin* compared to 56.9 percent of the *Inquirer* and 53.2 percent of the *News.*

f. By comparison, the *New York Times,* for one day (even though fifteen pages smaller than the average of the *Bulletin* and the *Inquirer*), ran slightly more local news than the *Inquirer–Bulletin* average, almost three times more national news, and more than twice as much foreign news.[6]

5. A survey of the front pages of both the *New York Times* and the *Los Angeles Times* for two-month periods in 1950, 1960, and 1969 (six months total) showed that stories about individual violent crimes were featured twice as often as stories about organized crime and three times as often as stories about white-collar crimes (price fixing, interstate violations, food and drug violations, etc.).

On the "Huntley-Brinkley" and "Walter Cronkite" newscasts for a two-month period in 1969, stories about individual violent crime were featured three times more often than stories about organized crime and seven times more often than stories about white-collar crime.[7]

ACTIVITIES

1. Define "important news" according to your own standards. Briefly explain why information telling that things are fine ("good" news) is not as newsworthy as information telling that something is wrong ("bad" news). Give one example of each.

2. List the advantages and disadvantages that television has in covering the news compared to those of a newspaper, news magazine, or radio.

3. Taking the first three pages of your daily newspaper, measure with a ruler the number of column inches devoted to local news, national news, international news, trivia, and advertising. The measurement should include headline and photo space. Make a chart comparing the amount of space given to each category.

Do you agree that the amount of space given to each category is about right? If not, which categories should receive more or less space?

As an alternate activity, do the same thing with your school paper using such categories as sports, social life, or education.

4. Examine the cover stories of fifty-two issues (one year) of a weekly magazine such as *Time, Newsweek,* or *Senior Scholastic.* Tabulate the number of cover stories devoted to different topics. What do you think of the magazine's news priorities as exemplified by its selection of topics? Were the covers chosen to emphasize important news, to arouse reader curiosity

and interest, to help promote or discredit a political viewpoint, politician, or cause, or to achieve a combination of the above?

QUESTIONS FOR DISCUSSION

1. Do priorities on coverage of entertainment, sports, and trivia tend to inflate the importance of games and entertainment at the cost of distracting the public's attention from more serious news? Does treating serious news on an equal level with sports, entertainment, and trivia make people feel that the serious news is not so important after all?

2. In your opinion, do news agencies pay enough attention to local, international, science, or education news? If not, spell out some of the reasons or difficulties involved. Whether you think the reasons are good or bad, what effect might distorted or inadequate news coverage have on the public's ability to support intelligent policies in these areas? Can you think of an example to prove your point?

3. Does an excess of sports, entertainment, and trivia news, combined with a shortage of the more serious news, tend to make people more or less apt to support a change in the status quo? Why?

17

Live Coverage

TEST CASE

The year: 1969. You are the president of one of the big television networks. What is planned as the largest demonstration against the war in Vietnam ever to be held is scheduled to take place this Saturday in Washington, D.C. Many famous people including entertainers, labor leaders, and U.S. senators will be there supporting the demonstration. It is called the "Vietnam Moratorium." Leaders predict that nearly a million people will show up and that the demonstration will be peaceful.

Will you give live coverage to this demonstration?

Compare your decision with the one that network executives actually made in this situation.

All three networks declined to cover the moratorium live. However, six months later all three networks and the Public Broadcasting Service, at the request of the White House, carried live some part of the "Honor America Day" demonstration supporting administration policy in Vietnam.[1]

A year earlier, CBS had called NBC News and ABC News ahead of time for the purpose of reaching an agreement not to give live or special coverage to the October 1967 Peace March on the Pentagon.[2]

Television coverage of such momentous national events as the first moon landing and presidential inaugurations provides every American the opportunity to share in a unifying experience. Nobody would question network decisions to carry them live. Nor would many find fault with the decisions to carry college and super bowl games live. The timeliness and excitement of these events make them especially suitable for live coverage, and this coverage brings in huge audiences and huge sums of advertising money.

However, not all decisions regarding live coverage are accepted without question. Some citizens dispute the wisdom of the networks in spending and losing millions of dollars for the coverage of presidential trips, additional trips to the moon, the return of prisoners of war or—on the local level—the installation of an archbishop. They ask further, if such events *are* covered live, why do all three networks need to do so at the same time, spending so much money to produce similar coverage? They point out that these events could be covered on a rotating basis and that the millions of dollars saved could be allocated to investigative journalism.

There are others who ask why live coverage wasn't given to huge political demonstrations and to sensational but significant Senate hearings on such issues as network news bias, prison brutality, the safety of birth control pills, and product safety. Others may have wanted to see live coverage of portions of the White House Conference on Hunger or conventions of the National Organization for Women (NOW) and the Consumer Federation of America.

The news consumer should question the priorities of live coverage just as he does the priorities of hiring, utilization of resources, and placement. For the consumer, it makes little difference whether bias results from the networks' political viewpoints, financial advantages, ideas of public service, or need to improve their own image. Without determining the motive, it is possible for the consumer to discover a pattern that is unifying the country behind some cultural events and symbols and not others. A biased pattern of live coverage would certainly be a matter of public interest, for it can be a powerful tool of persuasion.

MEDIA DECISIONS

1. In 1966, Fred Friendly, president of CBS News, resigned because CBS top executives overrode his decision to televise live the Senate Foreign Relations Committee hearings on the Vietnam War. CBS management felt the hearings were not important enough to justify preempting entertainment programs and thus lose advertising income. While CBS showed "I Love Lucy" and other entertainment programs, NBC covered the hearings live. Because of Friendly's resignation and the resulting criticism of the network, CBS resumed coverage. However, people in over seventy cities still could not view the full hearings because many NBC and CBS affiliates rejected the coverage.[3]

2. At a cost of over $2 million, all three networks covered live the sixth manned space trip (Apollo 16, April 1972) to the moon, allotting three evenings of prime time telecasts.

During the same month, a Senate committee was having a public hearing on the nomination of Richard Kleindienst for U.S. attorney general. These were lively hearings which focused to a large extent on the possible link between International Telephone and Telegraph's (ITT) pledge of $400,000 to help finance the scheduled Republican party convention in San Diego and the Justice Department's favorable out-of-court settlement of antitrust suits against the company. Another Senate committee was having hearings on, among other things, whether the Federal Housing Administration allowed speculators and finance institutions to reap large profits from the sale of FHA guaranteed homes. Meanwhile, in New York, the bloody prison riot at Attica was being investigated in public by the McKay Commission, a body established by the governor and the legislature of New York.

Although some public television stations in New York covered parts of the McKay Commission hearings live, the three networks had no live coverage of any of the hearings.

3. At a cost of some $3 million, all three networks carried live much of President Nixon's trip to China in 1972. Although the three planned to cover live the president's trip to the Forbidden City, CBS News president Richard Salant canceled CBS's scheduled coverage because he thought that the event lacked political significance. As Salant put it, "I just thought we'd had enough picture postcards" in the previous day's coverage.[4]

Later in the year all three networks carried live many hours of President Nixon's trip to the Soviet Union.

Nicholas Johnson, FCC commissioner, was very critical of the nation's new media for its live coverage priorities and especially for giving such massive coverage to President Nixon's trips.

4. For the first two days of live television coverage of the Senate hearings on the Watergate affair (May 1973), CBS, NBC, and ABC each lost $250,000 to $350,000 per day in advertising revenues. Neither NBC nor ABC carried commercials during their live broadcasts; CBS ran an average of only four commercial minutes per hour.

Within a week, the three networks agreed to rotate their daily coverage of the hearings. This allowed viewers a choice between the hearings or the regular daytime soap operas, games, and variety shows. At the same time the rotation reduced each network's advertising losses.

During the first two days, 9.5 million people nationwide watched the hearings during an average daytime minute, compared to the 13 million that watch regular network daytime programming. In some cities, such as Los Angeles, the more interesting days of the hearings attracted more viewers than regular programming.[5] Later, in the July 9–13 national Nielsen ratings, Watergate ranked number one.

5. At a cost of $3 million, all three networks decided to cover live the 1969 inauguration of President Nixon. An estimated thirty million people watched some part of the event. In prior briefings, NBC gave strict orders to its field producers, editors, correspondents, and camera crews not to cover or film any of the "counter-inauguration" demonstrations being held by antiwar groups.[6]

ACTIVITIES

1. Using a daily newspaper as a source of information, list three national events, conferences, or hearings that you think are important enough to be carried live on television. For each choice, briefly explain why you think it is important that the public be given the opportunity to view the event live.

2. Imagine you are the manager of a local television station and have decided to carry live two school events during the next semester. List the activities you would select in order of preference. State why you think each would be of value and interest to the community.

3. List all the events that you can remember seeing live on television during the last five years (excluding sporting events). Make a mark beside any of these events that seemed to you unimportant and undeserving of the cost of live coverage. Briefly explain why you think the event was undeserving compared to others.

QUESTIONS FOR DISCUSSION

1. Does the spectacular live coverage of a moon shot tend to increase public support for the manned space program?

2. Does live coverage of a presidential trip increase public support of the way a president is handling his job? Do you think that a president might plan a sensational trip just to get live television coverage? Could a number of these trips influence public opinion enough to make a difference in a close election?

3. Would a network of a very liberal, radical, very conservative, or far-right orientation decide to cover live the same events as the three moderately oriented networks? How much power is there in deciding for the American people what they will see live over television?

18

Pressure from Advertisers

TEST CASE

The year: 1972. You are the president of a major television network's news department. A seafood manufacturer claims that your news report covering a Senate investigation was not fair, that it gave coverage to critics who attacked the fishing canneries and their part in causing water pollution but that it refused to carry the industry's rebuttal given in testimony the next day. The seafood manufacturer has therefore told his advertising agency not to advertise over your network or affiliates, but instead to advertise over television stations that are more "hospitable vehicles" for such ads. Although you feel the report in question was fair, a lot of money is involved.

Do you intend to give the seafood manufacturer special treatment in your news in the hope that he will change his mind about withholding advertising from your network?

Compare your decision with the one that a network executive actually made in this situation.

CBS News president Richard Salant claimed that the coverage of the Senate investigation was fair, and that the fishing industry's rebuttal was ignored because CBS newsmen felt that a government report, which they did cover, gave the industry's side in a clearer, more per-

suasive manner than the industry's own rebuttal. Salant commented that Bumble Bee Tuna's withholding of advertising was unsophisticated and unreasonable. He commented, "I do not recall ever having been faced before with so blunt an attempt by advertisers to influence news handling and to punish a news organization."

CBS News did not change its news operation or policy in order to regain the advertising.[1]

The loss of advertising revenue is a serious matter for a news agency. Knowing this, some companies will threaten to withdraw their advertising unless a news story or policy that exposes or embarrasses them is suppressed or changed.

As a matter of pride and policy, most daily newspapers would defy such a blatant threat and print the story even if it meant a loss of advertising. Daily newspapers can afford to be courageous because they are in a strong position; they are usually the only daily in town and are secure financially. Furthermore, an advertiser may do more harm to himself than to the newspaper, because he will be depriving himself of the community's most effective single advertising medium.

Mass-circulation magazines and the networks are more vulnerable because an offended company can switch its advertising to a competing news agency and not hurt itself at all.

Most vulnerable to the advertiser's threat are the weekly newspapers. For them, a loss of advertising can spell the end of the paper. Many good and courageous weeklies such as the *Little Rock Gazette;* Lexington, Mississippi's *Advertiser;* the *Pecos* (Texas) *Independent;* Frederick, Colorado's *Farmer and Miner;* the *Morrilton Democrat* in Arkansas; *Cervi's Rocky Mountain Journal* in Denver; and Whitesburg, Kentucky's *Mountain Eagle* have either suffered greatly or been forced out of business because companies whose misdeeds they exposed withdrew advertising in retaliation.

For the news consumer, the loss of a good newspaper is a serious matter. But even more serious is the overall effect that fear of advertising loss has on news policies. In most cases, companies retaliate against news agencies quietly. Without admitting the real reasons, they can withhold, cancel, or switch their advertising. The message still gets across to the media owner. This is one reason why the mass media have traditionally assigned so few reporters and given so little attention to such topics as work safety conditions, product safety, and consumer quality. It explains why the restaurant, travel, and entertainment sections of many publications are more like promotional advertisement than critical review.

Some conservatives, however, don't see advertising pressure as a negative force. Instead, they think of it as a positive pressure that can be used to force news agencies to be more fair and to reduce what they consider to be the antibusiness propaganda of some news agencies.

In examining local newspapers and stations, a news consumer can often detect a bias resulting from the fear of advertisers if he asks which news policies and priorities, if any, might be affected by the fear of losing advertising. What kind of news agency could never get enough advertising to begin operation in the first place?

MEDIA DECISIONS

1. The *Financial Post* of Canada, a Maclean-Hunter publication, made some unfavorable editorial comments about the take-over of the Canadian Oil Company by Shell Oil in the early 1960s. As a result, the president of Shell Oil pulled all of his company's adver-

tising out of all Maclean-Hunter publications. The *Financial Post* did not change its editorial viewpoint in order to regain the advertising.[2]

2. Upon request, representatives of Coca-Cola Foods were given a preview screening of an NBC documentary, "Migrant," depicting Coca-Cola as one of the companies profiting from the exploitation of migrant workers in Florida. The president of Coca-Cola then called the president of NBC asking him to meet with Coca-Cola representatives before the telecast. The representatives asked for cuts in the program so that Coca-Cola would not be implicated as one of the companies responsible for deplorable housing and working conditions.

NBC accommodated, with minor changes. The president of Coca-Cola later testified that "Migrant" had correctly presented the deplorable conditions for migrants, and that his company was doing something to improve the situation.

Shortly after the program, in January 1971, Coca-Cola transferred a large amount of its advertising from NBC to CBS and ABC. That same month CBS News was criticized by some journalists for presenting a news story on Coca-Cola operations in Florida because it appeared to be an attempt at making the company look good.[3]

3. After a Jewish Defense League demonstration in front of the El Monte, California, Nazi headquarters in 1972, the *San Gabriel Sun* featured an interview with American Nazi lieutenant Joe Tommasi. Shortly after publication, several advertisers called and complained about the story, saying that it gave publicity to and legitimized the Nazi activities. A leading hardware store withdrew its advertising and threatened a general boycott.

Within a few hours the publisher of the paper sent out a flyer to all advertisers accusing his own reporter of bad judgment. The flyer stated:

And how we regret what happened in our issue of last week. . . . All I can say is that I am deeply sorry, and apologize to those who were offended by the article. . . . Rest assured that steps have been taken to make sure that no other "blown up" so-called news stories will ever appear in this newspaper.[4]

4. In 1969, the owner of three weekly newspapers, William Schanen, was warned by a prominent industrialist, Benjamin Grob, to stop taking contracts to print a Milwaukee underground paper called *Kaleidoscope* or face an advertising boycott of his own papers. Schanen refused, stating he had no right to censor another newspaper and that he should be able to accept whatever printing contracts he could get.

The boycott organized by Grob was immediately successful, causing Schanen's advertising revenue to drop from $4,000 to $700 a week. Because of the boycott, Schanen, one of whose Wisconsin weeklies had won a prize for excellence, was forced to sell two of his papers.[5]

5. A story in the *Nation* magazine revealed how the press responded in the 1960s when asked to cooperate in defeating the Hart Packaging Bill, a bill designed to take the deception out of the pricing and weighting of food products. The story related how the president of the Grocery Manufacturers of America visited the publishers of sixteen national magazines and afterwards recalled:

We suggested to the publishers that the day was here when their editorial department and business department might better understand their interdependency relationships as they affect the operating results of their companies; and as their operations may affect the advertiser—their bread and butter.

He was later able to point to press performances in eight magazines to show how well the publishers had paid attention to his message.[6]

Senator Philip Hart, sponsor of the bill, was scheduled to appear on television to discuss his bill, but his appearance was canceled. He was told, "off the record," that advertisers had objected.[7]

ACTIVITIES

1. Go through the daily newspaper or listen to a newscast and list all those stories that might have an adverse effect on the sale of a product. Look especially for stories about the quality or safety of a product or service.

2. Imagine you are the advertising director for a large company and have come to the conclusion that the local newspaper is printing articles that are unfair to your company and its product (select a product). Write a letter to the newspaper explaining and justifying why you are going to stop advertising in their newspaper until they give you fairer news treatment.

3. Imagine you are the president of a network news department and have just received a subtle hint from a large advertiser that if you don't cut down on news about the harmful effects of food additives, you will lose his company's advertising money.

Will you cut down on this kind of news to keep his advertising? If so, how do you justify such a decision?

If you decide not to give in to the threat, write a letter to the food company explaining why you will not or should not be influenced by this kind of threat.

QUESTIONS FOR DISCUSSION

1. Very often when an advertiser wishes to threaten or punish a news agency, he merely withdraws his advertising money. Although it may be obvious why he is canceling his advertising, he might not admit to using it as a lever to get special news treatment.

Does this make newspapers, magazines, and broadcasting stations shy away from covering news that may offend a large advertiser even before being threatened?

2. If a news agency does shy away from controversial topics or hard-hitting consumer stories, do you think the agency would admit their reasons? If not, how would they probably justify their action?

3. Can the subtle, unspoken influence of advertising on commercial news media be eliminated? If so, how? If not, why?

Books for Further Study

Barnouw, Erik. *The Image Empire: A History of Broadcasting in the United States from 1953.* New York: Oxford University Press, 1970.

Brown, Les. *Television: The Business Behind the Box.* New York: Harcourt Brace Jovanovich, 1971. What goes on inside the networks.

Mickelson, Sig. *The Electric Mirror: Politics in an Age of Television.* New York: Dodd, Mead & Co., 1972. From the viewpoint of a network executive.

Montgomery, Robert. *A Letter from a Television Viewer.* New York: James H. Heineman, 1968. A critical view from a former presidential adviser.

Shayon, Robert Lewis. *The Crowd-Catchers.* New York: Saturday Review Press, 1973. One of television's most respected critics takes a look at television.

IV

IN THE PUBLIC INTEREST

The Fairness Doctrine and the Equal Time Provision are often talked about and referred to by people who analyze or criticize the mass media. These laws apply to broadcasting only. They are embodied in the Communications Act of 1934 as interpreted and enforced by the courts and the Federal Communications Commission.

The Fairness Doctrine states that a broadcasting station, in its overall performance, must present the different, conflicting viewpoints on controversial matters in an equally forceful way. A station is required to give opposing viewpoints comparable opportunity to answer broadcasts that are advantageous to or include an attack on some person, group, or viewpoint. The doctrine applies to editorials, news and public-affairs presentations, presidential speeches and interviews, talk shows, and advertising. The doctrine was upheld by the Supreme Court in 1969.

The judgments as to whether or not the doctrine should apply in each particular case are left to network or station management. As a result, in many cases, there is much confusion and disagreement among complainants, broadcasters, the FCC, and the courts over just what the doctrine requires, if anything, to bring about fairness for all viewpoints.

For this reason, in discussing the test cases in the following chapters, interpret the Fairness Doctrine in the way that *you* think it should be interpreted to bring

139

about an equal and fair competition among all representative viewpoints.

The Equal Time Provision of the Communications Act of 1934 is an attempt by Congress to insure all legally qualified candidates for public office an equal opportunity to reach the public through the nation's airwaves. If a broadcaster gives any candidate free time or the opportunity to buy time, he must also offer the same to the other candidates for the same office. This provision is very clear in its meaning but there are still many official complaints concerning its application. Many people feel it doesn't insure a candidate an equal chance because it allows the wealthiest candidate to buy much more time than his opponents.

These regulations are based on the fact that broadcasters do not own the airwaves through which their television and radio messages travel. The Radio Act of 1927 and the Communications Act of 1934 clearly state that the airwaves *belong to the public*. There are also a limited number of frequencies available in any geographical area; not everyone may be given the freedom to broadcast. Therefore, it was thought best to give stations a temporary license to use the airwaves on the condition that they *serve the public interest*.

To do this a station must abide by both the Fairness Doctrine and the Equal Time Provision, and it must provide a variety of programming (including public affairs, news, editorials, chldren's programs), opportunities for local self-expression, development and use of local talent, and media services to community minority groups. The Federal Communications Commission evaluates the performance of each station every three years. If the broadcaster is found not to have served the public interest, his license can be taken away and awarded to another group or person that can demonstrate the intention and potential to better serve the public interest. As Judge Warren Burger stated in 1969, "A broadcast license is a public trust subject to termination for breach of duty."

But broadcasters have been able to ignore the public

interest and still keep their licenses because the FCC has for the most part served the interests of broadcasters instead of the public.

There are several reasons for this. First, because the FCC's authority and money to operate are given by Congress, it has considerable influence over the agency. It generally uses this influence to get the FCC to support what broadcasters want. No congressman wants to antagonize the radio and television station owners in his home territory for fear he might not get the good media treatment he needs for reelection. Second, the FCC members are appointed by the president. Most presidents have supported the dominantly commercial nature of broadcasting by failing to push for a strong noncommercial system such as that in England, Japan, Germany, and other European democracies. Former president Lyndon Johnson was a station owner himself. If a president is concerned about reelection, he is not going to appoint to the FCC individuals who are much opposed to the interests of commercial broadcasters. The network executive who is not happy with a presidential appointment is the same executive who decides whether opposing viewpoints will get to answer the president's prime time report to the nation. Many presidential appointees have in fact been previously connected with the broadcast industry. Third, some members of the FCC are subtly encouraged to support what broadcasters want because they know that if they please the industry, a good job in broadcasting might be offered them at the end of their seven-year term on the FCC.

The FCC has made some courageous rulings that have greatly displeased broadcasters (such as the ruling that the airing of certain controversial advertisements requires the station to provide free time for counter-commercials). But these rulings were usually badly needed minor reforms that in the long run probably helped more than hurt broadcasters. On the major issues involved in broadcasting policy, the agency has supported the status quo.

In the entire history of broadcasting, only three stations have had their licenses terminated because their programming was not in the public interest. Nevertheless, the airwaves belong to the public and the public has a right to demand that broadcasters provide, among other services, equal competition among ideas so that the individual American can make informed decisions about policies and politicians.

Keep in mind that since the public does not own newspapers or magazines as they do the airwaves, there are no laws requiring the print media to be fair, give equal space, or serve the public interest. The government reasoned that since anyone had the freedom to own and print a newspaper, this was guarantee enough that both free speech and a fair competition of ideas would prevail.

The President and the Fairness Doctrine

TEST CASE

The year: 1970. You are the president of a national network. The Democratic party chairman has asked your network for free time to respond to numerous reports to the nation by President Nixon, all of which were carried live by your network. The chairman claims that the Fairness Doctrine requires you to give him this time since many politicians and journalists agree that the president's speeches were partisan in nature and dealt with controversial topics. The administration claims the reports are nonpartisan.

Will you grant the Democratic party free time?

Compare your decision with the one that a network executive actually made in this situation.

Stating that CBS wanted to achieve fairness and balance to overcome "the disparity between presidential appearances and the opportunities available to the principal opposition party," Frank Stanton, president of CBS, granted Democratic party chairman Lawrence O'Brien twenty-five minutes to answer four specific telecasts by President Nixon. O'Brien made his presentation on 7 July 1970. The Republican party then demanded that they be given free television time to answer O'Brien. CBS rejected their request. The Republican party petitioned the Federal Communications Commission.

The FCC ruled that the Republicans should be granted their request. Both CBS and the Democratic National

143

*Committee appealed the FCC ruling. In November 1971,
a U.S. circuit court of appeals accused the FCC of "factual distortions and shifting justifications" in its process
of arbitrarily ignoring "the indisputable fact that the president, personally and through his spokesmen, had exten-
sively expanded the administration's views in numerous
television presentations."*

*The court therefore overturned the FCC ruling grant-
ing the Republican party time to respond to O'Brien's
speech. The court's decision seemed to broaden the area
in which the opposing party may demand air time to
include not only presidential speeches, but news conferences and comments by other administration spokesmen.*

*One circuit court judge stated that the FCC ruling had
given "one political party two bites of the proverbial
apple for every one granted to the opposition political
party." The result, stated a concurring judge, "strikes at
the heart of representative democracy and imperils the
very traditions upon which this nation is founded."* [1]

Nobody in the world at any time in the past or
present has had more persuasion power than the president of the United States. He can and often does talk
to as many as eighty million Americans in the intimacy
of their television rooms, and opposition spokesmen
are usually shut out completely.

The Fairness Doctrine attempts to counteract this
advantage by requiring the networks to give opposing
viewpoints comparable time to respond to presidential
speeches. But, it applies only if the speech contains
an element of partisanship. If the speech is solely a
report to the people from the head of state (for
example a declaration of war or of national emergency)
and if it doesn't include an attack on the opposing
political parties, then it is nonpartisan. However, if
the "report" in any way enhances the president's or

his party's policies or criticizes those of opposing parties, then it is partisan.

The decision as to whether opposing viewpoints will or will not be able to respond to the president's message has perhaps more impact on public opinion than any other single decision. Yet it is the top network executives—not Congress, journalists, or the public— who make this decision. If their decisions reveal a pattern of bias favoring the president or the opposing parties, they are contrary to the Fairness Doctrine, and to the public's right to a wide-open, robust debate on public issues of great importance.

In President Nixon's first four years in office (1969– 73) he received air time to talk directly to the people over television on more than fifty occasions. Only a few of these were judged partisan enough to require response from opposing viewpoints. When such time was given, it was given to the Democratic party alone, not to parties with viewpoints to the left or right of the major parties. The Republicans felt that many of the speeches answered were not in fact partisan and that therefore too much response time was given. The Democrats and minor parties felt that nearly all the president's speeches were partisan and that the networks should have given much more response time.

MEDIA DECISIONS

1. In a televised address to over seventy million Americans in November 1969, President Nixon pleaded for national unity and defended his Vietnam policy. The networks all judged that the speech was not partisan enough to require, under the Fairness Doctrine, that they seek out opposition party spokesmen to present their viewpoints. But the networks did allow some time for their own commentators to analyze the speech immediately after it ended.

A week later, Vice-President Spiro T. Agnew made his famous speech attacking the networks for their liberal bias and monopoly control over information. In attempting to prove his point, he mentioned the "instant analyses" as an example of how unfairly the networks treated the president. In Agnew's opinion, the president's speech was a nonpartisan address to the nation and as such shouldn't have been followed by either spokesmen for opposing viewpoints or by network commentators, "the majority of whom expressed in one way or another their hostility to what he had to say." [2]

2. In 1971, the Democratic National Committee requested free time under the Fairness Doctrine to reply to interviews of President Nixon by both the "Today" show (NBC) and Howard K. Smith (ABC). In addition, the committee requested time to respond to the president's Vietnam policy speech that had been carried simultaneously on all three networks. The networks turned down the requests.

In appealing to the Federal Communications Commission, the U.S. court of appeals, and later the Supreme Court, the committee was in essence asking that it be given reply time each time the president goes on radio or television. The committee stated:

> The president's unfettered access to television and its mass audiences to seek support for his programs and policies, combined with the inability of those opposing his programs and policies to obtain access to the same audiences, permits the president to dominate the discussion of controversial issues affecting the conduct of government.

The committee said that the Fairness Doctrine as presently interpreted by broadcasters "permits a broadcaster to limit the presentation of contrasting viewpoints to brief film clips on news programs, to responses to questions on news interview shows, or to the broadcaster's own editorial comment."

But by contrast, the committee added, the president "has total control over the timing, format, and content of the views he expresses on controversial issues." [3]

The court of appeals turned down the Democrats' request, stating that no interpretation of the Fairness Doctrine could be allowed to perpetuate a right to air time for responses to every presidential announcement in matters that are nonpartisan.

The Supreme Court's ruling in October 1972 upheld the court of appeals.

This ruling essentially maintained the status quo in the application of the Fairness Doctrine to presidential appearances by leaving decisions about application up to network executives.

3. The Black Caucus, a group of black congressmen, requested from all three networks free time under the Fairness Doctrine to reply to President Nixon's State of the Union address in January 1971. All three networks refused the request. The FCC also refused the request on the grounds that the issue discussed in the president's address had been fully covered by the networks. Later, the Black Caucus asked for free time from all three networks to present their documentary version of the "American Dream" in order to answer numerous presidential presentations. The caucus contended that network policies barring broadcasts not under the complete editorial supervision of the networks "violate the right of, and need for, self-initiated and controlled speech by nationally elected congressmen over the national TV media." They claimed that such policies violate the "public interest" provision of the Communications Act, the Fairness Doctrine, and freedom of expression under the First Amendment. All three networks refused the request. [4]

4. In April 1972, fifty persons rushed into the studio of WBZ-TV in Boston during a 6:00 P.M. newscast and

demanded that they be permitted to reply to President
Nixon's televised announcement about the war in Vietnam. During the ensuing confusion, in which forty-
four people were arrested for trespassing, the station
switched to commercials or displayed on camera a
"technical difficulties" card. The news audience was
not told about the happening.[5]

5. In March 1973, President Nixon was given prime
time to address the nation over all three networks. The
president attacked Congress for spending too much
money and he asked the people to write in support of
White House policies. The Democratic leadership in
Congress felt that the speech was partisan and thus
required, under the Fairness Doctrine, that the networks give them comparable television time to rebut
the president. Senator Edmund Muskie was designated
as the party spokesman; his speech was scheduled so
that the networks could easily cover it. All three networks refused the Democrats' request. This caused
House majority leader Thomas O'Neill, Jr., to state:
"I do not know whether the decision was merely poor
judgment by the networks, or whether the networks
were intimidated by the president's power to regulate
the uses of the airwaves." Whatever the reason, he
said, "the networks defaulted on their responsibility
to the public." [6]

ACTIVITIES

1. Define "partisan."
Imagine you are a local congressman who is making
a televised "Report to the Voter." In a partisan manner,
briefly write a report, or report orally, about three
different things you are doing in the nation's capital
to serve the voters. Report on the same activities again,
this time in a nonpartisan manner.

2. The next time the president speaks to the nation
over television or radio, note whether he makes any

partisan statements or whether he is merely making a nonpartisan report. List some of the statements that you think were partisan. In doing this, consider whether the address was such that it tended to support, directly or indirectly, one side or another of any controversial issue. Make a list of which issues and which sides he seemed to support.

3. Imagine that both the Socialist Labor party and the American Independent party, as well as the major party not in the White House, all want free time under the Fairness Doctrine to reply to what they consider a partisan speech by the president. If you were a network president and agreed that the speech was partisan, would you grant time only to the major opposition party or to all three parties? Briefly defend your decision.

QUESTIONS FOR DISCUSSION

1. Is it possible that what seems to be a partisan statement by one person may honestly seem to be neutral reporting by another? Can you find an example from a presidential speech or any other speech that is supposed to be only a report to the people?

Can any one person, no matter how experienced a journalist he is, interpret the Fairness Doctrine in a way that will be fair to or please all viewpoints? Design a better method than the Fairness Doctrine to insure that all representative political viewpoints and parties have a fair chance to get their word across through television.

2. When the opposing party is granted free time to respond to the president, the response is carried by only one station at a time. This allows the public to turn to two other network stations if they choose. On the other hand, when the president asks for and is granted television time to speak to the people, he is carried on all three networks at the same time, leav-

ing the public with little choice but to watch the speech. This results in a great advantage for the president. One presidential speech in 1971 reached 60 percent of the households; the opposition party's response to the speech reached only 9 percent. What can be done to remedy this built-in advantage?

3. Can a report to the nation be truly nonpartisan and still give an advantage to the president or to one side of an issue? If so, is it still fair to deny other parties time to respond?

How important and powerful are these decisions that decide whether anyone will be able to respond to the president? Is it conceivable that a pattern of decisions supporting the president, or the opposition party, might influence public opinion in such a way as to make a difference in a presidential election?

20

Advertising and the Fairness Doctrine

TEST CASE

The year: 1967. You are the manager of a large television station in New York City. An individual citizen requests that you grant free time for antismoking messages to balance great numbers of prosmoking advertisements that associate smoking with good health, success, and good times. He claims that since smoking is a controversial issue of public importance you are required under the Fairness Doctrine to present contrasting viewpoints. You are a bit surprised at this unusual request since no station has ever given free time for the presentation of antismoking messages. Though the case makes logical sense, you know that granting free time could establish a precedent that would antagonize your large advertisers and cost the station millions of dollars.

Will you grant free time for antismoking messages?

Compare your decision with the one that a station actually made in this situation.

CBS's New York City station, WCBS-TV, turned down the request. Lawyer John Banzhof then filed a complaint with the Federal Communications Commission. The FCC agreed with Banzhof and ruled that broadcasters conveying cigarette advertising must give "a significant amount of time" to anticigarette announcements. Not all stations complied. This brought Banzhof in 1969 to challenge the license renewal of several television stations on the grounds that they were violating the Fairness Doctrine.

Many more stations did comply, and as a result over $50 million worth of free antismoking commercials was aired per year until cigarette advertising over the airwaves was banned by Congress in January 1970.

The persuasive impact of a message is determined as much by the style and format of its presentation as by its content. This applies both to news and entertainment products, but it is best exemplified by advertisements. Their content often merely serves as a framework for the compelling words, imagery, associations, background music, and tone of voice that are designed to invoke a certain attitude from the consumer. It is difficult to measure exactly how effective an artistic advertisement is, but those who pay to have them made and aired are so convinced of their impact that they will pay as much as $200,000 to produce a one-minute advertisement and $30,000 to $60,000 for each showing on prime time television.

When such ads have a message dealing with such controversial issues as the auto manufacturer's concern for auto safety, corporate benefits for the Third World, the need for atomic power plants, or the environmental effects of lumber mills or strip mines, it gives an advantage to one side of an issue. Even ads that don't appear to touch directly on controversy may be promoting attitudes and life-styles that can be considered controversial. Many women's groups, for instance, have attacked seemingly noncontroversial ads for depicting women as subservient, product-oriented sex objects.

Others, including Nicholas Johnson, a former member of the FCC, claim that seemingly harmless ads for over-the-counter drugs are indirectly presenting only one side of an important issue:

There is a danger that our growing reliance on drugs may pose serious national health problems. . . . We could at least extend the Fairness Doctrine so that product advertising would be rebutted by counter-ads informing viewers of the adverse consequences of consuming the products at all.

But the FCC as a whole does not agree with this position, and a group of over-the-counter drug sellers has stated there is no validity to this claim since their own surveys indicate advertising has little impact on drug abuse.[1]

Recognizing that some ads can upset the balanced presentation of an issue, the FCC has made numerous Fairness Doctrine rulings to offset the advantage of advertisers. The rulings have required stations to give free time to groups with a viewpoint opposed to that of the advertiser. They can use this time to produce a "counter-ad." Broadcasters consider the counter-ad rulings a serious governmental interference with free speech as well as a threat to the economic basis of commercial broadcasting. Many citizen groups applaud the FCC rulings as a victory for the public's right to be exposed to competing viewpoints, each presented with relatively equal force.

MEDIA DECISIONS

1. Friends of the Earth, an ecology organization, asked NBC to broadcast information pointing out the harmful environmental effects of big cars and high-test gasolines in order to counter the advertisements that artistically depict the immense personality fulfillment that comes with the use of such products. WNBC-TV turned down the request on the basis that the Federal Communications Commission decision regarding cigarette smoking was not meant to apply to any other product advertising. The station also claimed that the advertising of cars and fuels was not controversial and that, furthermore, in several programs NBC had covered the topic of air pollution caused by automobiles.

The complaint was taken to the FCC which, in August 1970, ruled in favor of the station. The commission stated that if a commercial deals directly with an issue of public importance the Fairness Doctrine is fully applicable, but that to extend the doctrine to cover general advertising of products would "undermine the present system based on product commercials, any of which have some adverse ecological effects."

However, a United States court of appeals struck down the commission's support of NBC's decision. Agreeing with Friends of the Earth, the court extended the Fairness Doctrine to cover other products than cigarettes: "When there is indisputable evidence, as there is here, that the hazards to health implicit in air pollution are enlarged and aggravated by such products, then the parallel with cigarette advertising is exact." The court thus ordered television stations who carry advertisements for big cars and large horsepower ratings to broadcast information outlining the adverse effects of automobiles on the environment.[2]

2. The Television Information Office, an organization that speaks for broadcasters, bought spot advertisements that extolled the beneficial impact of television on children. Action for Children's Television (ACT), a public-interest group concerned with improving the quality of children's programming, requested under the Fairness Doctrine that the FCC order stations that ran the ads to carry an ACT counter-ad claiming that children's television is unimaginative, inartistic, commercial ridden, and harmful to children. The FCC denied the request in 1973, emphasizing that the doctrine requires that there be an overall balance on issues, and that ACT had failed to prove that the showing of the ads had created an imbalance.[3]

3. In its 1972 petition to the FCC to deny the license renewal of New York City's WABC-TV, the National Organization for Women claimed that the station's presentation of advertisements, as well as its pro-

gramming, was in violation of the Fairness Doctrine. The group stated that ABC failed to depict both sides of a controversial issue:

> The role of women in this society is a controversial issue, and while stations cannot be forced to cut out programs and commercials that show stereotyped views of women as housewives or as passive and dependent people, there must be a fair presentation of the other side of the question—that women are serious wage earners and are assertive and independent. . . .
>
> People tend to imitate roles they see to become what is expected of them. When they are given only one socially accepted "choice," it inhibits them from choosing freely what they want to be.

To support their case, NOW presented to the FCC the results of an extensive study of 1,241 commercials shown on the station. In 38 percent of the ads, women were depicted as demeaned housewives; in 40 percent, dependent on men; in 24 percent, submissive; in 17 percent, sex objects; and in 17 percent, unintelligent. In only 0.3 percent were women depicted as autonomous people, leading independent lives of their own. In contrast, the group found that men were depicted as independent, authoritative individuals, always engaged in some glamorous activity while the women tend the children and do the housework.[4]

The FCC denied the petition to revoke WABC-TV's license, but the complaint sparked minor reforms in both advertising and program policy.

4. The West Virginia state-owned and -operated Mountaineer Sports Network (twenty-five radio stations) devoted 25 percent of its total advertising time to ads by the West Virginia Surface Mining and Reclamation Association, a group of private mining companies. The ads defended strip mining and extolled the role of coal mining in West Virginia. In

October 1971, a coalition of black-lung victims, disabled miners, widows of miners, and opponents of strip mining asked West Virginia University (the network's operator) for time under the Fairness Doctrine to respond to the controversial statements in the ads. The station management in the flag station in Morgantown (WAJR) refused the request. The FCC supported the network's refusal by instructing the coalition to petition each individual station, not the network.[5]

5. Free time or space is given by mass media to governmental agencies and other organizations so they can advertise causes that are supposed to be noncontroversial and in the public interest. Such ads are called public service announcements (PSA). However, many critics argue that this gives big government and big business an unfair advertising advantage and that some PSAs do deal with controversial issues. For example, in 1970, about a thousand radio stations and nearly six hundred television stations ran free, as a public service, ads persuading viewers to buy a new car. Stations have also run, as a public service, ads depicting General Motors's help in establishing minority small businesses, ads for Radio Free Europe, and ads supporting a prisoner-of-war campaign to get people to send letters to Hanoi. At the same time, stations have refused to give free time for ads by nonpartisan organizations attempting to get college students to vote.[6]

ACTIVITIES

1. Watch a half hour of network-produced prime time programming on each of the three networks. List all the advertisements and note which ones contained a direct or indirect statement or visual image dealing with a controversial issue such as pollution, the role of women, use of drugs, conservation, or corporate responsibility.

2. Using your own idea of fairness, decide how many of these ads require that groups with opposing views be given free time to respond.

3. Select three of the ads that dealt with a controversial issue and write an opposing advertisement. On the left side of a sheet of paper write the narration and on the right side describe the type of film sequence and sound you would use to refute the original ad. If videotape or film is available, go on to produce your three counter-ads.

Or, do the above activities with radio advertisements.

QUESTIONS FOR DISCUSSION

1. What are some of the psychological or emotional rewards (such as respect) that advertisements offer the consumer if he buys a certain product or associates with a certain corporation? What are some of the negative consequences (such as rejection), that advertisements portray for the consumer who doesn't buy the right product? Apart from the product involved, can the depiction of a certain life-style or behavior as satisfying and rewarding be a matter of legitimate controversy?

2. For each of the rewards or consequences that you discovered above, what are some of the artistic techniques (words, symbols, music, imagery, associations) used to get the message across? To what extent have your own attitudes about consuming, sex, drugs, and social roles been influenced by these messages?

3. Of the following, which is the best policy regarding advertising and fairness? Why?
   a. No free time should be given to groups to respond to any ads.
   b. Ads containing direct or implied statements on controversial topics should be banned completely.

    c. For every ad touching on a controversial topic, free time should automatically be given to opposing viewpoints.

    d. Maintain the present policy giving the broadcast executives the power to decide whether an ad requires free time for opposing viewpoints under the Fairness Doctrine.

21

The Equal Time Provision

TEST CASE

The year: 1972. You are the president of a network television news department that has recently had the two leading candidates for the Democratic presidential nomination, George McGovern and Hubert Humphrey, appear on an interview program. Two other officially recognized candidates for the same office ask your network for equal time. They claim that the interviews of McGovern and Humphrey were, in reality, debates rather than legitimate news interviews and, as such, amount to a gift of free debate time. The candidates therefore claim that the Equal Time Provision of the Communications Act requires that your network give them broadcast time equal to that given to McGovern and Humphrey.

Will you give equal time to the two candidates who are requesting it?

Compare your decision with the one that the networks actually made in this situation.

All three networks refused to give equal time to presidential candidates Sam Yorty and Shirley Chisholm because, in the networks' judgment, the interview programs were not debates or grants of free time to McGovern and Humphrey but were bona fide news interviews. Coverage of bona fide news events or interviews are exempt from requirements of the Equal Time Provision, whereas debates or grants of time are clearly covered.

The Federal Communications Commissions agreed with

*the three networks by deciding that the interview pro-
grams in question qualified as bona fide news events. On
this ground they dismissed the petitions by Yorty and
Chisholm.*

*Yorty then took his case to a federal court in San
Francisco. The court dismissed his case on procedural
grounds.*

*Chisholm took her case to the U.S. circuit court in
Washington, D.C. The court decided that the networks
and the FCC were wrong, that the CBS and NBC interviews of McGovern and Humphrey were in reality debates, that therefore the Equal Time Provision required
CBS and NBC to give thirty minutes of free prime time
to Chisholm, and that ABC's forthcoming interview of
McGovern and Humphrey must also include candidate
Chisholm. CBS and NBC gave time to Chisholm as ordered, but they did not give any time to Yorty or to
George Wallace, who was also actively campaigning,
because the court did not demand it. However, ABC
enlarged its forthcoming interview program to include
Yorty and Wallace as well as Chisholm.*[1]

To prevent an unfair advantage in elections, European democracies forbid a candidate's buying broadcast time. Candidates appear on public-affairs programs
or are given an amount of time in some proportion to
their party's representation in the legislature.

In the United States, there is no such restriction; a
candidate is free to buy considerable chunks of broadcast time regardless of whether his opponent can afford to buy any. In 1972, a new election law demanded
disclosure of the names of those contributing over $100
to any political campaign. The new law also limited
paid political advertising in the mass media to no
more than ten cents per person eighteen and over.
However, this law still allows the wealthier candidate
to gain a tremendous advantage, especially if his opponent cannot match the limit.

In selling time to candidates, the broadcaster is required under the Equal Time Provision to offer each the same opportunity to buy time. Very few candidates have occasion to file complaints, for very few broadcasters would even think of violating this requirement. However, there are many complaints based on the provision's second requirement—that stations give each candidate for the same office an equal amount of free time. When a reporter interviews a candidate or reports on his statements, the station considers this a news or public-affairs program, not a grant of free time. But the other candidates, the FCC, or even the courts may consider that the program was in effect a grant of free time. Complaints filed with the FCC that charged stations with unfair treatment under the Equal Time Provision totaled 2,764 in October 1972 alone.

Broadcasters oppose the Equal Time Provision and claim that they would grant more free time to the *major* party candidates if they didn't have to grant an equal amount to all the minor candidates. Minority parties claim this would be unfair, for it would allow broadcasters to give an enormous advantage to the major parties, with whom they are usually in agreement, and it would deprive the voters of exposure to all qualified candidates and their viewpoints.

The news consumer should consider whether the present provision provides an equal opportunity for candidates and what might be a better alternative.

MEDIA DECISIONS

1. During the 1972 presidential campaign, the Communist party, Socialist Workers party, and Republican party requested equal time to balance network time given to George McGovern's announcement of Sargent Shriver as his running mate. They claimed that the announcement was not a bona fide news event because only sixty-one seconds of the sixteen-minute

speech was devoted to Shriver, the rest being partisan statements about different issues in the campaign.

The networks refused the requests, claiming that the announcement was an important and bona fide news event and therefore not covered by the Equal Time Provision. The Federal Communications Commission also refused the petitions for equal time, agreeing with the networks that the announcement was a legitimate news events.[2]

2. The American Independent party received 14 percent of the popular vote in the 1968 presidential election. In the 1972 election, the party filed a $25 million suit against the three television networks, charging "a virtual news blackout of the party's campaign" that had resulted in severely impairing the election efforts of candidate John Schmitz. The suit claimed that the news coverage by the networks is "not news at all but, on the contrary, reflects a multimillion-dollar contribution to the Republican and Democratic parties," and as such is illegal. The suit charged that the

> blackout of the American Independent party was a gross violation of Federal Communications Commission regulations, requiring equal air time for all candidates from opposing political parties.

Commenting on the suit, candidate Schmitz said, "I'd take distorted coverage over no coverage." [3]

3. NBC television gave thirty seconds of free broadcast time to both John Ashbrook and Paul McCloskey, candidates for the 1972 Republican presidential nomination. The two candidates had requested the time under the Equal Time Provision to balance candidate Pat Paulsen's short appearance as an actor in a movie shown by NBC. The network acted after the FCC had ruled that Paulsen's appearance on television—even as an actor—entitled other candidates to equal time. The thirty-second announcements were run during station breaks on the "Saturday Night Movie." [4]

Ed Nelson, actor and candidate for city councilman of San Dimas, California, has a twelve-minute role in NBC's "Rod Serling's Night Gallery." Nelson's five opponents demanded equal time under the Equal Time Provision. KNBC-TV in Los Angeles gave each of the five men equal broadcast time to promote his candidacy. To preclude this from happening again, KNBC canceled future shows in which Ed Nelson had a part. Nelson then withdrew from the race for city council in time enough for the station to go ahead with the original plans to air the shows.[5]

TV Guide commented editorially that interpretation of the Equal Time Provision to cover a candidate's appearance as an actor was ridiculous because the actor was not appearing as a candidate. It added that equal opportunities for all candidates should, in this case, only demand that other candidates be free to pursue an acting career.[6]

4. The Las Vegas television affiliate of CBS refused to carry a half-hour nationally televised paid political speech of Senator George McGovern on 10 October 1972. The station claimed it was not violating the Equal Time Provision because it was rejecting all political speeches over sixty seconds, thus giving equal treatment to all candidates.[7]

Numerous stations, including WTEN-TV Albany, KSD-TV Saint Louis, WHED-TV Rochester (N.Y.), WTIC-TV Hartford, WBAP-TV Dallas, WMAL-TV Washington, D.C., and WMAR-TV Baltimore, also refused to carry the same McGovern speech. However, ten days later these stations carried a half-hour paid announcement supporting President Nixon. Another station guilty of affording such unequal treatment, WNEW-TV New York City, justified their actions by stating that after they turned down McGovern they changed policies in midstream due to programming and financial considerations. Thus, in theory, they did not violate the Equal Time Provision since the policy in effect at the time of such announcement was applied equally to all candidates. But in practice, the change of policy resulted in unequal opportunities.[8]

5. During the presidential campaign of 1964, President Lyndon Johnson gave a television address to sixty-three million Americans in which he explained the significance of recent international events—the fall from power of Russian premier Nikita Khrushchev and the Chinese atomic bomb tests. He said these events necessitated a firm but reasoned and steady posture on the part of the United States.

Both the Republican party and the Socialist Workers party demanded equal time to reply. Republicans claimed that the speech was of "an obvious political nature" since their candidate, Senator Barry Goldwater, held views on foreign policy and nuclear strategy that were central issues during the campaign.

ABC and CBS refused to grant the requests; NBC offered equal time to the Republican national chairman, Dean Burch, the following night. The FCC upheld the networks' refusals on the grounds that the president's address was a legitimate report to the nation on a crisis situation and therefore was not partisan in nature. Burch, who five years later was appointed head of the FCC, stated that the FCC ruling in this case violated "every purpose and intent of the laws governing the airwaves." [9]

ACTIVITIES

1. Briefly defend the network practice of giving vastly more news coverage to the two major party candidates and almost ignoring the minor party candidates.

Or, defend the minor parties' contention that the networks should cover all candidates equally rather than on the basis of whether—according to the networks—they are responsible or have a chance of winning.

2. Imagining you had never heard of the Equal Time Provision, write a law that you feel would equalize broadcast opportunities for all candidates.

3. Define what you think is a "bona fide" news event as contrasted to a political announcement. Give examples of each.

QUESTIONS FOR DISCUSSION

1. How would political broadcasting be different if there were no Equal Time Provision? Would broadcasters be inclined to give major party candidates even more of an advantage than they already have? In how many states should a minor party candidate for president have to qualify before he merits better news coverage? Who should decide these matters: Congress, broadcast executives, or the FCC?

2. Is it fair that the wealthiest candidate be allowed to buy more television and radio time as well as newspaper space just because he has more money, or should the purchase of such communications advantages be prohibited or severely limited as it is in European democracies? How might these different policies affect what type of candidates there are and what programs they advocate?

3. Since broadcasters and newspapers earn so much money from political advertising, would it be realistic to expect them to cover the issue in an unbiased way, or to crusade for the elimination of paid political advertising?

Books for Further Study

Barret, Marvin, ed. *Survey of Broadcast Journalism.* Annual. New York: Grosset & Dunlap.

Johnson, Nicholas. *How to Talk Back to Your Television Set.* New York: Bantam Books, 1971. Ways of evaluating a station's performance and forcing them to improve programming—by a former FCC commissioner.

Minow, Newton. *Equal Time: The Private Broadcaster and the Public Interest.* New York: Atheneum, 1964. By a former head of the FCC.

Morris, Norman. *Television's Child: A Report for Parents.* Boston: Little, Brown & Co., 1971.

Skornia, Harry J. *Television and Society: An Inquest and Agenda for Improvement.* New York: McGraw-Hill, 1965. A case for change by a former president of the National Association of Educational Broadcasters.

V

BALANCING THE MARKETPLACE
OF IDEAS

Representatives of minority viewpoints may have the right to free speech, but at the same time they may be deprived of a real chance to get public support for their ideas or interpretations. Of course, they can speak on a street corner or perhaps get published in a small magazine, but 99.9 percent of the people would not be exposed to their ideas. Without equal access to the mass media they compete for public acceptance at a tremendous, if not insurmountable, disadvantage.

It is certainly unfair when any representative viewpoint is excluded from the mass media or, for financial reasons, can't compete on an equal basis with other viewpoints. But for the individual consumer of media products, it is far worse than unfair treatment. It can amount to the deprival of his freedom to think, for if he is exposed to an unfair competition of viewpoints it means he is not being given a real choice. In essence, he is being deprived of the opportunity to make up his own mind.

Unfair competition among all representative viewpoints is called "imbalance." A newspaper or station that hires only moderate liberals and moderate conservatives is imbalanced.

A magazine that publishes only radical writers and

articles is just as imbalanced as a radio station that carries only far-right public-affairs programs.

A news program is imbalanced if it allows commentaries from liberal or conservative journalists but excludes those from radical, very liberal, very conservative, and far-right journalists.

The news consumer should be concerned about the degree of imbalance within particular programs, magazines, newspapers, or stations. But, if the lack of balance in one news agency is countered by an opposing imbalance in another comparable news agency, the total information product presented through the mass media will be balanced even if particular publications or stations are not.

Whether this overall balance has been achieved through a commercial communications system alone is an issue of vital importance. Since the owners, managers, and their hired editors and producers cannot deny that they are the ones who make the important decisions, they must claim to be making these decisions fairly for all viewpoints—even ones they detest. Otherwise, they cannot say there is a balance or a fair competition of ideas. The final section of this book explores in greater detail the question of balance.

22

Selecting Sources of News

TEST CASE

The year: 1971. You are the news director of a local television station in a northern Midwest city. The Ford Motor Company has invited you to spend "a couple days in the Florida sun" in mid-December while covering a two-day "news conference" on what Ford has termed a "significant business and social development": the boom in recreational vehicles. Air flight and other expenses will be paid by Ford. Ford will also provide four sound-camera crews to help you cover the event.

Will you accept the invitation?

Compare your decision with the one that many station managers actually made in this situation.

Among the 43 out of 100 stations that accepted the offer were stations in Detroit, Indianapolis, and Buffalo. Another 27 stations were unable to accept Ford's invitation, but they requested from Ford footage of the event for use in their newscasts.[1]

A news agency can't print or broadcast information it doesn't receive. What information it does receive will be determined by the news sources it depends on and the news policies it adopts. These are both owner or top-level executive decisions which are very important in determining the balance of a news agency's product. If its major sources of news all have a similar political orientation, and if it restricts the use of other sources for additional information, then the final products will inevitably be imbalanced.

The international wire services are the primary sources of hard news. The Associated Press and the United Press International are the largest; together they supply about 75 percent of all television and radio news. Besides these two, a news agency can subscribe to the British Reuters, the Agence France-Presse, the Dispatch News Service, and the Liberation News Service. There is a significant difference in the subject matter and bias of these wire services.

Syndicates and news services provide special news and numerous features such as background analyses, columnists, editorials, cartoons, comics, entertainment news, and travel pieces. King Features, National Enterprise Association, and the U.S. Press Association are three large syndicates that provide hundreds of syndicated features. The *New York Times, Los Angeles Times, Washington Post,* Newhouse, Gannett, and Copley news services emphasize columnists, analyses, and background news.

In addition to the above sources, a publication or station can use information coming directly from citizens' groups, union or company public relations offices, advertising agencies, and government officials and agencies in the U.S. and other countries. Much of the material supplied by these sources is already written or filmed in the form of a news story. The news agency can thus use the material without having to change it. Finally, a news agency may have its own investigative reporters.

The problem of which source to depend on in wartime is crucial for both the wire services and the individual news agencies. American reporters in Vietnam get most of their information from military sources, not from on-the-spot observations. As many former military public information officers have testified, by the time the reporter gets the information, it has been censored by going through five or six channels of the military information machine.[2] Furthermore, the reporter is encouraged to accept the Pentagon version: he is given accreditation, briefings, easy access to officers, swimming pool and bar privileges, PX rights, free air flights, interpreters, and a chauffeured jeep. When a reporter's stories contradict or displease the Pentagon he will likely have some or all of these privileges revoked.

Few would claim that the stories coming from enemy or neutral sources are any more reliable or less biased than the official administration or Pentagon version. But to ignore such stories as a matter of policy is a limiting journalistic practice, as was made evident by the My Lai massacre story during the Vietnam War. The National Liberation Front (NLF) news sources, both radio and print, described the massacre pretty much as it happened soon after the event, but at this time American news agencies had a policy of ignoring enemy sources; thus, they all reported the Pentagon version of 126 enemy soldiers killed—when in fact hundreds of civilians had been killed. (See test case, Chapter 8.)

Because so much of the official information about Vietnam later turned out to be false or misleading, some American news agencies in the 1970s began printing stories coming from European, North Vietnamese, and NLF sources. These American news agencies pointed out that to do so was not to be disloyal or to support a neutral or enemy viewpoint; but rather, it was fulfilling the journalistic responsibility to publish pertinent information from every source so that the American public could best ascertain the facts.[3]

News policy also determines whether and how a publication, station, or wire service will cover "staged" events. A staged event is one that is put on for the sole purpose of getting news coverage. A press conference is, of course, staged. A demonstration may be partly staged.

A news consumer should be aware of what sources a particular publication or station has at its disposal. He or she should also attempt to determine the limitations, characteristics, and biases of the different sources.

MEDIA DECISIONS

1. A survey of the *Washington Post* revealed that it devoted most of its attention to official proceedings of the government, government information handouts, and scheduled events. The survey showed that only 5 percent of the stories in the newspaper were the "original" or "enterprising" type—stories resulting from the initiative of the newspaper itself.[4]

A survey of all six New York City television station evening news programs in January 1971 showed that during a four-day period 85 percent of the news items had appeared on wire services or in newspapers prior to being aired and that only 6 percent of the total time was devoted to enterprise or original reporting. One random sampling revealed that nine of fourteen news stories covered by the stations on a particular day were staged news conferences and demonstrations.[5]

W. Phillips Davison, professor of sociology at Columbia University, found in a survey that public relations sources (including government information sources) originate between 40 and 60 percent of the news found in the daily and weekly press.[6]

2. The Pentagon is a prime source of news and various productions for radio, television, and newspapers. Most of this material, provided at no charge, has a direct or implied bias supporting the Pentagon version of foreign and domestic policies and events. The army's hometown news center in Kansas feeds information to 1,700 daily and 8,300 weekly newspapers, and to 2,700 radio and 550 television stations. In 1970, the army's series "The Big Picture" was being shown on a regular basis by 313 commercial and 53

public television stations. Many local television stations showed the air force's "V-Series" newsfilm documentaries—some of which were staged—that supported the past and current views and activities of the Pentagon in Vietnam. Fourteen of the thirty "V-Series" newsfilms released between October and December 1969 promoted the administration's "Vietnamization" program. Some stations showed these films as news without labeling the source.

The State Department and the National Aeronautics and Space Administration also produce programs that are regularly requested and aired by a large number of radio and television stations.[7]

3. About 1,600 of the nearly 1,775 daily newspapers in the United States depend entirely on the AP and UPI wire services for foreign news coverage. In turn, the wire services in most cases obtain more of their information from the government and press of each foreign country than they do from their own investigations.

4. News agencies have long accepted the rules of "background briefings" given to journalists by government officials: reporters at the briefing, or using information gained at the briefing, should not disclose from which official they got the information. Instead, they are to identify their source as "a top official" or "an administration spokesman."

The *Washington Post* broke the backgrounder rule in 1971 by revealing that it was Henry A. Kissinger who told them that President Nixon might reconsider his plan to visit Moscow if the Soviet Union failed to work for peace between India and Pakistan. Benjamin Bradlee, executive editor of the *Washington Post*, stated that he did so to "get this newspaper once and for all out of distributing the party line of any official of any government without identifying that official and that government. . . . We have engaged in this deception and done this disservice to the reader long enough."[8]

5. On 13 September 1971, state police forces assaulted the state prison in Attica, New York, in an attempt to free hostages held by rebellious prisoners. A total of forty-one prisoners and hostages were killed in the assault. It was reported that the prisoners had killed several hostages by slashing their throats with knives. The *New York News* featured the story under the headline: I SAW SEVEN THROATS CUT. The other news agencies also reported the story of the slashed throats. But within a day a medical exam proved that this story was false, that the hostages had not had their throats slashed, but rather had died of shots fired by the state police.

The source of the original story was the prison officials. However, seven out of eight major news organizations checked carried the story of the slashed throats as established fact without naming their source.[9]

ACTIVITIES

1. Write a news report about what happened in your classroom during the day using only the information given you by the teacher. Find out what was covered by the teacher, how the students reacted, and what they did.

Then write a news report about the same classroom, this time using only information given you by other students.

Finally, write a news report about the same classroom using only yourself as a source of information.

Compare the three, noting differences in the story resulting from the use of different sources.

Make audio or videotapes of the above news stories instead of a written report.

2. Analyze two articles on the front page of your school or daily paper. List the information sources used by the reporter.

3. Go through your daily newspaper or monitor a local newscast and list the articles that you suspect originated from a public relations source in a union, corporation, travel bureau, government office, or other organization. State briefly why you suspect or know each story to have originated in some public relations office.

QUESTIONS FOR DISCUSSION

1. Is information from persons in positions of authority always the most reliable? If a reporter knows that an official is lying, should he still report the official's statements objectively without comment or analysis?

2. Should a newspaper refuse to print a story that doesn't give the name of the official who is the source of the story? Why? If a story printed on page 1 is found to be false, should a correction or retraction also be printed on page 1?

3. Should a journalist, newspaper, or network use every available source in an attempt to arrive at the truth, or should they, as a matter of policy, disregard information coming from enemy sources, or from sources they don't like?

4. If a news agency depends totally or primarily on established news sources such as the government and the wire services instead of its own reporters, to what extent is it merely serving as a channel for the official version of the events? Given the dependency on these sources, will the news products of radio, television, newspapers, and weekly magazines be very similar in overall perspective, priorities, and bias? If so, is the uniformity of news a good or a bad thing? Why?

23

Hiring

TEST CASE

The year: 1969. You are the manager of a television station. Along with all other television and radio stations in the country you have been ordered by the Federal Communications Commission to eliminate discrimination in your employment practices. Although you feel that your employment practices are based on practical and professional considerations rather than on any conscious or unconscious bias, a check of your station's personnel shows that you hire no blacks, Chicanos, or women in professional roles such as reporter, writer, news producer, or photographer.

Do you feel that you need to change your employment practices in order to comply with the FCC order? If so, what changes or practices will you institute?

Compare your decision with the ones that stations actually made in this situation.

A large percentage of radio and television stations have done little or nothing to comply with the FCC order to eliminate discrimination in employment practices. This was made evident nearly three years later when a Justice Department official, Ben Holloman, stated that the broadcasting industry had "one of the worst records" in the country in the employment of minorities. Accusing the broadcasters of "tokenism," he went on to say that "a few black faces on the television screens hide the *fact that there are few members of minorities behind the cameras and practically none at executive levels."* [1]

FCC actions in 1972 and 1973 also revealed that many stations were doing little to end discrimination against blacks and women. In an attempt to enforce its ruling, the FCC held up the license renewal of thirty television and radio stations in Pennsylvania and Delaware and of fifty-nine stations in Florida because they appeared "to be in non-compliance" with the FCC order banning discrimination.

The FCC actions may have been partly prompted by the communications coalition of black groups who had earlier asked the FCC to investigate the hiring and promotion practices at twenty-eight of Philadelphia's thirty-six stations. The coalition claimed that of 1,448 people employed by the city's broadcasters, only 57 professional positions were held by blacks even though there is a substantial black population in the city.

Can a conservative owner or executive make major news decisions and policies in a way that is fair to all representative viewpoints on the political spectrum?

Can a news agency that hires only liberal journalists consistently present the views of radicals and far rightists in a fair manner?

Can white, male, middle-class executives and journalists make decisions that allow the ideas of women, blacks, and other minorities to be presented fairly?

Can one top-level executive, without sharing power or consulting with journalists representing different viewpoints and cultures, establish news policies and priorities that are fair to all?

If so, then a news agency can produce a balanced product whatever its hiring practices may be.

But if individuals, because of their political views, sex, and cultural backgrounds, are unable to be fair to every other viewpoint and culture, then news agencies need to hire qualified people of different viewpoints and backgrounds in order to present balanced news.

Ownership naturally determines hiring patterns. As late as 1972, blacks owned none of the nearly 700 commercial television stations, 15 of the 7,000 commercial radio stations, and 4 of the 1,750 daily newspapers in the United States. In the same year, a study by the American Society of Newspaper Editors found that of 40,000 professionals working for daily newspapers, only 253 (less than 1 percent) were blacks or members of other minorities. There were only 8 minority group individuals in executive positions.[2]

Covering the years 1971 and 1972, the most extensive study ever made of employment in the television industry found that 70 percent of the commercial television stations were "pure white" in managerial positions; 50 percent employed no racial minorities in professional capacities; and 18 percent employed no women in the top four job categories. Public television showed a similar racial imbalance, but a better record regarding employment of women—at least in the lower echelons. The governing boards of public stations were composed almost exclusively of white men. Of 125 public stations responding to the survey in 1972, 44 employed no minority group members on a full-time basis. In the top job categories (officials, managers, professionals, technicians), 52 stations employed no minority group members, and 18 percent employed no women.[3]

To detect a bias that might be the result of hiring practices, a consumer can try to imagine how different the news product would be if qualified people of different political viewpoints, sexes, races, and cultural backgrounds were hired.

MEDIA DECISIONS

1. Austin Scott, the first black reporter hired by the Associated Press (1961), resigned in 1972 in pro-

test against what he considered the AP's tokenism. Thanking AP for the great treatment and exceptional opportunities they gave him, Scott nonetheless wrote to Wes Gallagher, the general manager of the wire service, that this treatment was

> also one of the reasons I'm resigning. We now have . . . 18 black reporters, none of whom have had anything like the chances AP has offered me. And as I've said to you and others in repeated letters, I think the time for tokens passed long ago.
>
> Once I'm gone, AP will have only three ways to deal with the black community stories that I cover, from black politics to welfare to the Panthers: ignore them, send in white reporters, or bring more black reporters along faster. . . .
>
> In any case I think I will have done the AP good by stepping aside, whether I help stop the pretense that we have done what we should or help us to move faster.[4]

2. McGraw-Hill, Inc. received approval from the Federal Communications Commission in 1972 to buy television stations from Time-Life Inc. despite complaints by minority coalition groups that the sale violated FCC policy by perpetuating monopoly ownership of television licenses. The minority groups then took the case to the U.S. court of appeals. But the case was dropped when the coalition reached an agreement with McGraw-Hill that for each of the four stations purchased it would:

a. Establish a minority advisory council to serve as a principal consultant in developing minority programs from topics and format to talent recruitment and training.

b. Show, in prime time, a substantial number of programs dealing with minority interests and achievements of both Chicanos and blacks.

c. Establish employment policies assuring that within three years 15 percent of the employees would be from minority groups, and no fewer than 25 percent of these employees at each station would be in professional, managerial, sales, and technical positions.[5]

In May 1972, a coalition of black public-interest groups gained similar concessions from two of the three network-owned television stations in New York City. The CBS-owned station refused to work out similar agreements, stating: "While WCBS-TV welcomes and seeks out suggestions from interested individuals and groups, management responsibilities cannot be shared." [6]

3. To balance three regular syndicated columnists whose viewpoints were liberal or very liberal (Tom Wicker, Anthony Lewis, and James Reston), in 1973, the *New York Times* hired William Safire, a conservative and one of President Nixon's speech writers.[7]

4. In his study of network news operations, Edward Epstein found that all television networks hired correspondents who had similar profiles. Most were originally from a small midwestern city, studied speech, drama, or English, and received quick job promotions. Few had any long-standing connections with political or social organizations or political causes—a major factor in their being hired, for the networks excluded from consideration those who were biased, committed, politically involved, activists, dogmatic, or advocates. Epstein found that their political viewpoints on major issues were not liberal (as commonly alleged by Nixon administration spokesmen), but varied between moderately liberal to moderately conservative. On many issues they took a detached nonideological viewpoint.[8]

5. A study was undertaken by a group of newspaper editors in 1964 to determine which columnists were most likely to be hired by newspaper syndicates and news services. Columnists were listed under three categories on each side of the political spectrum. The "very conservative" columnists made up 29 percent of the

1,861 columns classified, compared to 1 percent for those termed "very liberal." Going toward the middle of the spectrum, "conservative" columns accounted for 20 percent compared to 8 percent for "liberal" columns. The columns taking a position near the middle of the road, written by "mildly liberal" or "mildly conservative" columnists, made up 42 percent of the total.[9]

ACTIVITIES

1. Imagine that your school paper has no black reporters even though blacks constitute 20 percent of your school population.

Decide whether you think your school newspaper should use a quota system to guarantee that minorities will be represented according to their enrollment or whether the paper should select reporters solely on the basis of writing experience and merit even if this might mean there will be no minority group reporters. Write a letter to the editor supporting your position on this issue.

2. Imagine that in your school Chicanos make up 10 percent and blacks 20 percent of the student enrollment. The two minorities and the 70 percent white enrollment each seem to prefer different types of music played over the school public-address system at noontime.

Design a plan so that during a four-week period each group has a fair opportunity to present its own musical program hosted by its own disc jockey.

3. Watch a local television station's half-hour evening news program for five straight days and keep a record of how many different reporters, newscasters, and weathermen appeared. What percent was white, black, Chicano, female? From your findings would you say that this station is making an effort to abide by the FCC's ruling outlawing discrimination in employment practices? Briefly summarize each commen-

tary or "news analysis" given during the five days. Classify each according to what political viewpoint it seemed to support (liberal, conservative, very conservative, etc.).

QUESTIONS FOR DISCUSSION

1. Can a white reporter communicate what it's like to live in a ghetto or on an Indian reservation as well as a black or Indian reporter of equal talent? Why?

Can a male reporter communicate what it's like to grow up in a male-dominated society as well as a woman reporter of equal talent? Why?

Can a reporter who grew up in a large northern city communicate what it's like to grow up on a farm as well as a reporter with a rural background?

2. What are the chances that a moderate commentator or newscaster will present a so-called extreme viewpoint (on the left or right) without using some kind of bias, verbal or nonverbal (such as facial expression or tone of voice), to disparage or ridicule the viewpoint?

If you feel this type of bias can't be eliminated, how can a news agency, by its hiring policy, make sure all viewpoints are depicted fairly?

3. Do you feel that, if exposed to contradicting ideas from all political viewpoints, sexes, and minorities, the public will be too confused to make intelligent choices? If so, which viewpoint, sex, or race should be in charge of managing the different viewpoints so that the public will choose the "right" one and not be confused?

24

Firing

TEST CASE

The year: 1971. You are the manager of a radio station. One of your reporters has stated over the air that none of the businesses in the town's main street are complying with the federal government's price freeze requirement to post a list of ceiling prices in a conspicuous place. He mentioned by name the stores not complying. Some of these stores advertise regularly over your station. They are disturbed by the report. One client has canceled his advertising and others are threatening to do so.

Will you stand behind your reporter or fire him in order to prevent further cancellation of advertising by local businesses?

Compare your decision with the one that a station manager actually made in this situation.

James Lange was fired by station WQWK-FM in State College, Pennsylvania, after giving his report on the failure of businesses to post price ceilings. The station manager claimed the report was unfair to local businessmen and that Lange didn't "clear" the story. Lange claimed the news director okayed the story in advance. After being fired, Lange complained to the Federal Communications Commission; and Consumers Union publicized the case. Soon afterward, Lange was reinstated as a reporter.[1]

Sometimes the firing of a journalist is justified; sometimes it is not. A single firing may not seem too important in itself, but it communicates to other journalists that certain practices, opinions, investigations, or presentations will not be tolerated. Since journalists naturally want to keep their jobs, few will perform in a way that would threaten their security. Others will not even apply for work at a particular news agency because the firing of a like-minded journalist will have convinced them they won't be welcomed by the management. This cautiousness on the part of journalists affected by a firing cannot but influence the news.

The firing of certain journalists may help explain why so many newsmen and news programs seem to be alike. It may also indicate the limits of criticism tolerated by the mass media. In general, criticism of specific bad conditions, persons, or institutions is more easily tolerated by management than criticism of the political, economic, or communications system as a whole.

MEDIA DECISIONS

1. In the late 1940s, William L. Shirer's news program was dropped by CBS for what they said were programming considerations, but Shirer was sure the move was an attempt to silence him for his liberal ideas. At the time he had an audience of over six million.

Shirer's suspicions were not unfounded. In the years following World War II, anti-Communist groups pressured sponsors and networks to drop many liberal radio commentators, or to slash their air time. At least twenty-four suffered such fate in 1946 alone, including Orson Welles, Henry Morgenthau, Max Lerner, James Roosevelt, and Fiorello La Guardia. The anti-Communist groups were especially upset by commentaries that seemed sympathetic to organized labor or to the Soviet Union, and by discussions of the political power of the Catholic church, business monopolies, or "dollar diplomacy." One of the most famous commentators, Drew Pearson, was fired by his radio sponsor when Senator Joseph McCarthy, a leader of the anti-Communist movement, threatened the sponsor with retali-

ation if Pearson remained. Such retaliation usually
meant that the sponsor would be accused of being a
Communist sympathizer.[2]

2. William Woestendiek, editor of WETA-TV's
"Newsroom," was fired in 1970 because his wife went
to work for Mrs. John Mitchell, who was the wife of
the attorney general of the United States. The New
York station felt that Woestendiek's wife's employment would create a conflict of interest, making it
difficult for him to report objectively on issues affecting
the attorney general. Three contributing editors of the
program resigned to protest the firing. They contended
that Woestendiek's wife's job would not prevent him
from reporting in a professional manner.[3]

3. Ted Hall, the managing editor of the Passaic-
Clifton *New Jersey Herald News,* was fired in 1969
when he refused his publisher's orders to stop investigating a murder case involving charges against the son
of a publisher of a nearby suburb newspaper.[4]

4. Dr. Martin Abend was a regular commentor on
WNEW-TV's nightly evening news program. In the
spring of 1969, nineteen of twenty news employees of
the New York City station petitioned the management
to have Abend ousted for his "purely" and "extremely"
far-right commentaries. It was claimed that his strong
bias would damage the entire news staff's reputation
for objectivity and fairness. The station did not reply
to the petition, but it did restrict Abend's commentaries
to less popular programs on the weekends.[5]

5. The city editor of the Waterbury, Connecticut,
Republican, Floyd Knox, was fired for running, on
Vietnam Moratorium day in 1969, a front-page list of
Vietnam War casualties from the Waterbury area.[6]

ACTIVITIES

1. List three people that you know personally who
were fired from any kind of job they may have had.

For each one, find out the management's official reason for the firing. Did the persons fired believe that the official reason was the real reason? If so, did they think it was a good enough reason? If not, what do they think was the real but unstated reason for their being fired?

2. Imagine that you are James Lange, the journalist described in the test case. Write a letter of protest to the station manager. Then write another brief letter that you will pass out to people in the community or try to have published in the newspaper.

3. Imagine you are the editor of your school newspaper. Write an employment policy spelling out the kind of reporter behavior or writing that could and should result in dismissal.

State two or three pressures (personal, financial, or political) that might prompt an employer to fire a reporter unjustly.

QUESTIONS FOR DISCUSSION

1. Have you ever said something just to please the boss, thinking that it might get you a job or keep you from getting fired? Have you ever written something you didn't believe just to get a better grade from a teacher? Can you imagine a situation where a journalist might stifle, temper, or change what he has to say or report because of similar considerations?

2. What does the following statement have to say about the hiring and firing of reporters or commentators: "The person who is careful in hiring won't have to resort to firing." Could it apply to a journalist's political ideas as well as his capacity to do his job?

3. Since the firing of a reporter or editor can affect what information or viewpoints people will receive, should a station or newspaper owner be required to justify the firing in front of a citizens' committee?

Editorial Endorsement and Bias

TEST CASE

The year: 1972. You are the editor of a daily news-paper. Which of the nine presidential candidates are you going to endorse on your editorial page: Richard Nixon, Republican party; George McGovern, Democratic party; John Schmitz, American party; Benjamin Spock, People's party; Louis Fisher, Socialist Labor party; John Hospers, Libertarian party; Linda Jenness, Socialist Workers party; Gus Hall, Communist party; or Harold Munn, Prohibition party?

In your news reporting of the campaign, will you in any way favor or give special treatment to the candidate you endorse?

Compare your decision with the one that daily news-papers actually made in this situation.

Richard Nixon received endorsements from 753 daily newspapers; only 56 papers endorsed George McGovern. One Communist daily newspaper supported Gus Hall and one conservative daily supported John Schmitz, but none of the other presidential candidates received even one endorsement. An independent stand was taken by 245 papers. Although the support given Nixon was over-whelming, the majority of newspapers usually endorse the Republican candidate. In 1948, papers accounting for 80 percent of daily circulation supported the Republican, Thomas E. Dewey; and only 10 percent supported the Democrat, Harry Truman. In 1952, 80 percent backed

Republican Dwight Eisenhower against 10 percent for Adlai Stevenson, the Democrat. Stevenson got 10 percent again in 1956, and Eisenhower received endorsement from 60 percent. In his first try for the presidency in 1960, Richard Nixon reecived 71 percent compared to John Kennedy's 16 percent; and in 1968 Nixon again received more newspaper support in terms of circulation than his opponent, Hubert Humphrey, by a five-to-one margin. Only in the 1964 election did most of the normally Republican press endorse the Democrat, Lyndon Johnson, over the very conservative Republican, Barry Goldwater, by more than a three-to-one margin.[1]

Nearly every newspaper owner or editor claims that the personal opinions of the management are restricted to the editorial column and that the news columns are free of bias. Nevertheless, nearly every scholarly publication and journalism review indicates that in a large percentage of newspapers, editors gave preferential news treatment to the politician or viewpoints endorsed on the editorial page.

Some journalists and owners claim that editorial endorsement has no effect on public opinion and is therefore of no advantage to a candidate. They point out that many candidates endorsed by the press have lost. Other journalists claim that endorsements have a considerable influence on public opinion. They point out that just because a candidate who wasn't endorsed won an election, this does not prove endorsements have no effect. The candidate might have won more easily and by an even greater margin had he been endorsed.

A news consumer will want to consider both arguments as well as the question of who should decide on endorsement. In the 1972 presidential campaign, some endorsements were made by the editorial staff and some by the publisher. In one case James Cox, the owner of ten newspapers, including the respected

Atlanta Constitution, ordered all of his papers to endorse the candidate he favored.

MEDIA DECISIONS

1. The January 1973 issue of the *Columbia Journalism Review* published the results of a study on how fairly the press covered the Watergate scandal—one of the major stories of the 1972 presidential campaign. The study deals only with the earlier period of Watergate disclosures, not with the later stages in 1973 when new disclosures brought about maximum newspaper attention and live television coverage of Senate hearings. Examining thirty major newspapers, the study found that those endorsing President Nixon minimized or refused to print the Watergate disclosures at a much higher percentage than those that made no endorsement for president.[2]

A classic 1956 study of how newspapers handled particular stories about Richard Nixon, then Republican Vice-Presidential candidate, and Adlai Stevenson, the Democratic Presidential candidate, showed that thirty-five of the thirty-six papers included in the study gave more favorable news coverage to the candidate they endorsed on their editorial page.[3]

2. John S. Knight of the *Detroit Free Press,* a respected publisher who did not favor Barry Goldwater for president in 1964, admitted that most of the media (which endorsed Lyndon Johnson) were unfair to Goldwater's campaign: "I do think the Arizona senator is getting shabby treatment from most of the news media." Talking about the columnists, he commented that there are "only a few who are not savagely cutting down Senator Goldwater day after day," and that cartoonists portray him "as belonging to the Neanderthal Age, or as a relic of the 19th century." He went on to say:

Some editors are disturbed because Barry Goldwater is teeing off on the newspapers and other news media for failing to present the news of his candidacy fairly and objectively. I can't say that I blame him. He hasn't had a fair shake.[4]

3. A national survey of small daily newspapers and weekly papers showed that in the early 1960s, 84 percent took an editorial stand against any government-sponsored medical or hospital aid to the aged. The vast majority were also opposed to federal aid to education.[5]

4. In 1967, the *Boston Globe* analyzed the editorial positions taken by thirty-nine of the nation's major newspapers on the subject of the war in Vietnam. Four papers took a position on the far right and called for an all-out win policy. Sixteen supported the Johnson administration policy without reservation. The remaining nineteen took a moderately conservative or moderately liberal position by supporting the United States commitment but favoring deescalation and increased peace efforts. None were against the commitment or called for an immediate withdrawal of U.S. troops.[6]

5. A study, by Congressman Bob Eckhardt in 1971, of nearly one hundred of the largest newspapers showed that the two-thirds of the newspapers that regularly endorse Republican candidates also endorsed the conservative position on the ABM system, the Carswell Supreme Court nomination, the Cambodian invasion, the McGovern-Hatfield antiwar amendment, and Spiro Agnew's statements against dissenters.

ACTIVITIES

1. Write an editorial endorsement of the candidate you would like to see elected as the next student-body president at your school.

2. Check to see who the weekly or daily newspaper

endorsed for a major office in the last local election in your community. Over the period of time covering the campaign, compare all the stories about the candidates to see which candidate, if any, got more and better photographic treatment, more and better headlines, and better placement.

3. Aside from the reasons given in the editorial of your local newspaper, try to determine or gather information as to why the newspaper's publisher or editor endorsed a certain candidate. For example, are the publisher and the candidate personal friends? Do they belong to the same country club or church? Are their sons in the same little-league team? Does the candidate favor policies or construction projects that might affect the varied financial interests of the publisher or of his major advertisers? Does the publisher stand a chance to be appointed by the candidate to some city committee or agency?

QUESTIONS FOR DISCUSSION

1. Which do you think is most effective in persuading the public to vote for a candidate—an editorial endorsement, or a long-term hidden bias giving one candidate better photographs, headlines, and placement?

2. Which is more important in influencing public opinion—the bias at election time, or a twenty-year bias supporting a liberal or conservative orientation toward politics, economics, and society?

3. Could overall newspaper bias conceivably influence enough people to make a difference in an election? If so, is this a situation a democracy can tolerate? Are there ways to have newspaper endorsement and bias balance out fairly?

Some candidates win elections even though they have less editorial support and money for advertising than their opponents. Does this mean that newspaper bias and money are not important?

26

Achieving Balance

TEST CASE

You are the managing editor of a monthly magazine that claims to be fair and nonpartisan. It serves as a digest of important articles from various other magazines.

On any one controversial issue over a long period of time, are you going to make an effort to select articles representing all viewpoints, or will you select mainly those articles that you agree with?

Compare your decision with the one that a mass-circulation digest actually made in this situation.

From 1950 through 1969, the Reader's Digest presented 84 articles dealing with Vietnam. Of these, 81 supported U.S. policy in Vietnam, and 3 were neutral.

During the same period, the Digest selected 99 articles favorable to U.S. foreign policy and corporate activity in Latin America compared to 2 unfavorable and 10 neutral articles.

From 1950 through 1959, the Digest sided with investor-owned electric power companies against customer-owned power companies. It published 9 articles dealing with the issue; all 9 either praised the private power companies or attacked the customer-owned companies and the government policies that made them possible.

The concept of socialized medicine was criticized in 9 articles from 1945 through 1959 without any articles in support.

The labor movement, from 1952 to 1965, received 49 critical articles contrasted to 8 favorable and 5 neutral.[1]

Broadcasting stations and newspapers try to serve everybody; they claim their news products are balanced. Most magazines aim their format, editorial content, and advertising toward a special type of reader and usually admit to representing a particular political viewpoint, value system, or interest. This lack of balance does not necessarily detract from the value or quality of a magazine. What does detract is the use of bias hidden under a pretense of balance. Since bias is so often hard or even impossible to detect, the public can be convinced it is getting a balanced presentation when in fact it is not. For the citizen, it doesn't matter whether a newspaper, station, or magazine is biased to favor a particular viewpoint as long as the bias is known and there are comparable agencies to present alternate biases.

Of course, every viewpoint cannot be presented; there are thousands of them. But most individual viewpoints fall within a spectrum of representative thinking that can be divided into four or six categories depending on the issue involved. If a viewpoint is so peculiar that it has no representative publication, has no qualified political candidates, and can obtain no scientific, scholarly, or traditional support to back it up, then it need not be considered representative. It can be ignored without sacrificing the public's right to be informed.

But if a viewpoint has its own publication, qualified candidates, and scholarly, scientific, and traditional support, then the people should hear it, even though it is unpopular. In the course of history, unpopular ideas have often emerged as the soundest in the long run. But they may be ignored if they are not presented to the public through the mass media.

Does "balance" mean that every position must be

given equal weight? Some television programs have in fact been canceled because the host, after a reasonable effort, couldn't find anyone to support one side in a controversy. The host claimed a cancellation was necessary because he couldn't create a fifty-fifty balance, pro versus con.

Such a mathematical approach indicates a complete misunderstanding of balance. For example, if only one out of six representative viewpoints proposes a return to slavery or a repeal of income taxes, then a presentation of these issues could be weighted five to one against these proposals and still be balanced. A fifty-fifty presentation in this case would be unfair and deceiving. Of course, on most controversial issues, only two or three viewpoints would be lined up on each side of the question.

The information consumer should not only be concerned about getting balanced news products through the mass media, he should also be concerned about all the people in all communities across the nation receiving a balanced and wide-open debate on all the issues.

MEDIA DECISIONS

1. During a six-month period in 1969 just prior to the Senate's narrow approval of the antiballistic missile system, the *Los Angeles Times* did not print any of eleven news stories that spelled out significant opposition to the ABM, even though the stories were carried by wire services to which the *Times* subscribed. Other daily newspapers considered some of these stories so significant that they featured them on the front page. The stories told of opposition to the system by the Federation of American Scientists, senators, the president of the Ford Foundation, 3,200 scientists and scholars, 76 percent of the 1,216 physicists in the American Physical Society, and 13 Nobel Prize winners including a former White House science adviser.[2]

2. On one Sunday in June 1970, during the controversy over President Nixon's order to move troops into Cambodia, the network interview programs had eight liberals scheduled for appearance compared to no conservatives.

On one evening's late-night shows in January 1970, the four talk shows hosted by Dick Cavett, Johnny Carson, David Frost, and Merv Griffin had a total of four guests critical of the U.S. policy in Vietnam compared to one supporting it.[3]

3. An interview program hosted by Martin Agronsky and carried by several public television stations in the East was monitored by Accuracy in the Media, a group concerned with fairness. They found that over a two-month period in 1972, 80 percent of the programs featured guests who were wholly or predominantly liberal or antiadministration. In contrast, only 10 percent were wholly or predominantly proadministration or conservative.[4]

4. Public Broadcasting Service's "Week in Review," during the 1971-72 season, regularly had five journalists discussing the significance of the week's events. All five were members of well-established liberal or conservative news agencies. Journalists from far-right, very conservative, very liberal, or radical publications never appeared on the panel.

CBS's "Special on the Pentagon Papers" was a panel discussion chaired by two moderate CBS reporters and featuring three journalists and three politicians. No one more liberal than Max Frankel of the *New York Times* or more conservative than Texas senator John Tower was represented. There was no representation of the radical, very liberal, and far-right viewpoints regarding the Pentagon Papers and their significance.[5]

5. Programs produced by such individuals or groups on the far right of the spectrum as H. L. Hunt, the Reverend Carl McIntire, the American Security Coun-

cil, and Billy James Hargis are carried over 10,000 times a week on over 1,700 radio and numerous television stations.

In contrast, the far left—made up of such groups as the Communist party, the Progressive Labor party, the Students for a Democratic Society, and the Socialist Workers party—has a few hundred outlets a week on only a handful of radio stations.[6]

ACTIVITIES

1. Select a topic of public importance that interests you. Examine three years of the *Reader's Digest* (thirty-six issues) to find all the articles on this topic. Read the articles and classify them as for, against, or neutral.

Do you think the *Digest* was fair in its selections? If you feel some sides of the controversy weren't represented adequately, list other magazines that are likely to better represent those sides of the controversy.

2. Examine any magazine's advertisements or articles and then describe the type of person you think that magazine is aimed toward.

3. Take a subject that might be very controversial at your school (such as dress codes, smoking on campus, mandatory attendance at assemblies, lunchtime passes, free speech), and find articles dealing with this subject in the last five copies of the school newspaper. Classify the articles as for, against, or neutral. If one side seems to have an advantage in the amount of space or interviews given, can this be justified on the basis that few or no groups or students could be found to support the other side?

4. Imagine you are to set up a four-person panel discussion on a controversial topic at your school. First, list four class members who all hold slightly different views that you consider reasonable.

Then list a new panel that includes one person to represent every position on the issue even if you consider some viewpoints extreme, dangerous, irresponsible, or obscene.

Which panel do you think would be the fairest? Which would be the most interesting to listen to? Why?

QUESTIONS FOR DISCUSSION

1. Suppose that for every five wire service articles a newspaper receives indicating that the oceans are becoming more polluted, there is only one article stating that the oceans are not so bad and are in fact getting cleaner. In checking the sources of these articles, you find that all viewpoints are represented; it just appears that most agree on this analysis.

How should an editor utilize these stories in order to achieve what you would consider a balanced presentation?

2. Does the mere act of excluding from panel discussions spokesmen with extreme positions make people think such spokesmen and their viewpoints are not responsible?

If all the panel members seem to be debating each other, does this necessarily mean that all viewpoints are represented? Does such a debate make the public believe that all sides are represented?

3. If some groups are advocating the legalization of an illegal practice such as gambling, prostitution, or hard drug use, should the news media publish only those articles that advocate the present legal position, or should articles be published on both sides of the issue?

Books for Further Study

Aronson, James. *Packaging the News: A Critical Survey of Press, Radio, TV.* New York: International Publishers Co., 1971. A study by a former newspaper editor showing the degree of cooperation between the government and mass media—from a radical viewpoint.

Bagdikian, Ben. *The Effete Conspiracy: And Other Crimes by the Press.* New York: Harper & Row, 1972. An experienced journalist and press critic examines the issue of how liberal or conservative the press is—from a liberal viewpoint.

Cirino, Robert. *Don't Blame the People: How the News Media Use Bias, Distortion and Censorship to Manipulate Public Opinion.* New York: Vintage Books, 1972. From a very liberal viewpoint.

Efron, Edith. *The News Twisters.* Los Angeles: Nash Publishing Co., 1971. A study of network news bias during the 1968 presidential campaign—from a very conservative viewpoint.

Koegh, James. *President Nixon and the Press.* New York: Funk and Wagnalls, 1972. A study of bias in the press's news treatment of President Nixon—from a conservative viewpoint.

Lokos, Lionel. *Hysteria 1964.* New Rochelle, N.Y.: Arlington House, 1965. A study of anti-Goldwater bias in the 1964 presidential election—from a very conservative viewpoint.

A CONSUMER'S VIEWPOINT

How often did your response to a test case agree with the decision actually made by the media executive or journalist? You probably disagreed on quite a few occasions. You may think that in some cases the person who made the decision did so purposely to keep certain information from the public in an attempt to create, reinforce, or change public opinion. You may be entirely right, for there are many cases of deliberate slanting or censorship of news, entertainment, and advertising that take place every day in both broadcasting and print media. But there are many more media executives and journalists who make decisions based on their honest judgment of what the people should know and *not* on what they would like the people to believe. Nevertheless, even among these honest and dedicated journalists there are often disagreements about which decision is correct. And more important, their decisions may have as much influence on the public as the decision of a journalist or media executive who deliberately sets out to manipulate public thinking.

In other words, what counts most is the kind of bias and quality of information people are receiving in spite of the fact that most media executives and journalists have good intentions. Similarly, what counts most is the safety of your car or the purity of your food, not the good intentions of the auto manufacturer or the butcher. The journalist, automotive engineer, and butcher can all be honest, dedicated, and professional, yet their decisions can still result in the production of inferior products.

For this reason, in defining key words, analyzing media decisions, looking for causes, and proposing solutions, it is advantageous to study the problem of bias in the mass media from the vantage point of a consumer instead of that of a producer.

What differences in thinking occur from this new vantage point? First, any single information product that is arranged to favor one viewpoint is seen as propaganda. It is propaganda even if the producer didn't intentionally arrange it. To communicate one has to select certain topics and facts at the expense of others. To do so inevitably favors some viewpoints over others. In addition, the selection or use of a particular style of presentation can favor a viewpoint even more than the selection of information. The choice of a word, headline, placement, photograph, film, tone of voice, posture, or facial expression can intentionally or unintentionally embellish or detract, exalt or ridicule the viewpoints and events presented as the content of news. Information products are propaganda whether they include truth and reason on one hand or lies and inconsistencies on the other. Under this definition every information product qualifies as propaganda: to communicate is to propagandize. Thus, the usual debate about what is and isn't propaganda, and who is and who isn't a propagandist, can be eliminated. The propaganda controversy will then be elevated above the level of calling the opponent a propagandist and will be focused on the quality or type of propaganda. That is, whether or not any particular piece of propaganda is truthful, reliable, verifiable, and relevant to the understanding of oneself and society. The issue is not whether there is propaganda or not, but whether the public is receiving competing propaganda from all representative viewpoints.

Propaganda is dangerous to the public at large only if there are a limited number of counteracting propagandas of equal technical and artistic force. When different propagandas are balanced against each other, then the public has a real choice.

We all grow up speaking a language that is different from most other people's. This greatly influences the way we look at the world. We also relate to other people and to the environment in different ways. Each individual—even within the same country—has gone through different emotional experiences. In short, every human being is influenced by, and inseparable from, his past experiences with family, culture, subculture, language, and social class.

Our selection and interpretation of information is very much affected by these human experiences; they can't be eliminated. Without these influences our brains and body would not grow or be healthy; we would not become human beings. As a result, we are all biased in one way or another. There is nothing wrong with being biased as long as the bias isn't so extreme as to sacrifice facts, reason, flexibility, or relevance. Realizing this, the consumer's viewpoint does not bother with the question of whether someone is biased or pay serious attention to those who accuse others of being biased. People should be applauded for admitting their bias. Those who hide under a pretense of objectivity or detachment should be persuaded to admit their biases. This is no easy task, for those with media power gain a great propaganda advantage by claiming to be objective—they can promote their own viewpoints without the public being aware of it. This pretense enables those in power to refuse opposing viewpoints the equal opportunity to produce news and allows them not to be called to task for it.

Beneath every claim of objectivity, or of being in the "middle," there is some bias. As former FCC commissioner E. William Henry said, "The middle position isn't *no* position, it is a position." Objectivity or the middle position usually contains a bias supporting established power and authority. For example, to report objectively what the president, a senator, the Pentagon information office, a corporation president, or a union leader tells you—when you know it is a lie or at best a deception—is to be biased in favor of established authority. The decision to depend on established information sources, rather than on other sources, is a biased decision. As *New York Times* reporter Tom Wicker noted, the practice of objectivity is an act of advocacy favoring the status quo. Everyone and every communications product has a bias; the real issue is whether the public is receiving just one or two kinds of hidden bias under a pretext of objectivity or is receiving the openly admitted biases of many different cultural and political viewpoints.

If media executives and journalists admit their biases, they will have to concede that they have an unfair advantage and, thus, allow those with different biases an equal chance to control and present information. To take an obvious example, mass media has been and is staffed primarily by white middle-class journalists who—purposely or unconsciously—communicate a bias much more respectful of whites and white culture than of nonwhite races and their cultures. This incontestable fact forces any fair-minded journalist at least to admit the prowhite bias or, better, to place nonwhites in decision-making positions so that they can counteract with bias of their own.

Censorship is usually defined as a *deliberate* act of withholding information for moral or political reasons. This definition is totally inadequate and misleading from a consumer's point of view. What counts in a democratic society is that the people are being deprived of information. Therefore, to a consumer, *any decision, practice, or assumption that results in the people being deprived of points of view or information whether in news or entertainment—regardless of reasons or intentions—is censorship.* Applying this definition to the test cases, you can see that many of the decisions made by media executives and journalists actually amount to censorship. The rejection of an advertisement, documentary, or story, and the refusal to sell broadcast time result in the people being deprived of information just as much as the more open censorship of the stories of the My Lai massacre, of the United States preparation to invade Cuba, or of the buildup of ground troops in Vietnam in 1965.

Again, the question is not whether censorship decisions are being made, but whether they counteract or support each other. If all three networks (NBC, ABC, CBS) and the two wire services (UPI and AP) censor or ignore a story or situation, there is little chance that the majority of people will get this information. But, if one of the networks or wire services handles a story, then the censorship decisions made by the others will be counteracted. The information will get out and the other agencies will be forced to cover the story or lose credibility and prestige.

The most important question for a democracy is whether there is, among those who produce, control, and disseminate information products, enough diversity to create a counterbalancing effect. If this counterbalance exists, then the existence of propaganda, bias, and censorship will not prevent the people from making up their own minds. Not only will there be fair competition among viewpoints, but the quality of information products will be improved. A communicator is not so likely to use shoddier techniques of propaganda such as lying, name-calling, misquoting, unfair selection, and appeals to prejudice if he fears his techniques will be exposed and his credibility destroyed. He will not so readily censor information if he fears that he will be caught or that his competitor will be praised as an enterprising and courageous media executive for breaking a story.

Counteracting propaganda and bias are of little help to the vast majority of citizens and to our democracy if they exist only in books, "underground" publications, small-circulation magazines, or scholarly journals. Counterbalance must exist *in the mass media* in order to be effective both in influencing the performance of journalists and in giving people a real choice. Of course, small-circulation publications are of great value to those few individuals who have sufficient time and skill to locate and read them. On many occasions articles in these publications force the mass media to disclose previously censored information or to give attention to a situation that has been ignored. However, by the time this happens, the information may no longer be timely or relevant to decision making. The damage may have been done.

From 1964 to 1967, public support of the U.S. policy of ground combat escalation in Vietnam was based largely on censored information that was not counteracted in the mass media. The majority of Americans later withdrew their support when the opposing point of view began to appear in the mass media. The tragedy is that this counteracting propaganda existed in minor publications from the very beginning. However, it was of little value to the majority of people and to our democracy because the information wasn't where it counted—in the mass media.

After the U.S.-sponsored invasion of Cuba in 1961, which ended in defeat of the anti-Castro forces at the Bay of Pigs, President Kennedy said that had the mass media done its duty it would have saved the nation from this illegal undertaking. He told the *New York Times*'s managing editor: "If you had printed more about the operation, you could have saved us from a colossal mistake." He later added: "I wish you had run everything on Cuba. . . . I'm just sorry you didn't tell it at the time." [1]

Opposing viewpoints must be available over an equal length of time in order to be effective in helping people select the most just, reasonable, and humane policies. The person who has been exposed only to racist, integrationist, capitalist, or Communist propaganda throughout his early adulthood will not readily reexamine his ideas as soon as he is exposed to counteracting propaganda of equal artistic force. If there is fair competition among different viewpoints on only one out of seven days, or in one out of twenty years, there is imbalance. Balance implies fairness over a long period or fairness in the total product of a newspaper, network, or system, not just in a single article or program.

But just what is fairness? As applied to communication in a democracy it refers to a condition where all representative viewpoints on the political spectrum have an *equal opportunity* to convince the public that their facts, interpretations, and ideas are the most truthful, relevant, and responsible. However, there is a considerable difference of opinion on what constitutes an equal opportunity. Media executives and journalists believe they can provide this opportunity by making decisions (such as you made in response to the test cases) and by presenting people's viewpoints in such a nonbiased, professional, or detached manner that no side will have an advantage over any other.

The government also believes this. Its tool for encouraging and demanding an equal opportunity for all viewpoints is the Fairness Doctrine. As you may have come to realize, this doctrine has three obvious shortcomings. First, it doesn't apply to newspapers or magazines. Second, the doctrine leaves it up to journalists and media executives to make the decisions that will provide the equal opportunity. And third, the doctrine is seldom used as a means of promoting an equal opportunity in advertising or entertainment. This last shortcoming is by no means insignificant, for over a long period of time the overt or implied messages in advertising and entertainment have a profound impact on public attitudes. Censorship of television entertainment and advertising has been taken for granted from the very beginning. How widespread that censorship still is was revealed in February 1972 by David W. Rintels, chairman of the censorship committee of the 3,000-member Writers Guild of America. He found that 86 percent of guild members had experienced censorship of their work, that 81 percent believe that television is presenting a distorted picture of what is happening in this country today, and that only 8 percent believe that current television programming is in the public interest. He related that writers have "proposed shows about South African apartheid, Vietnam, old folks, mental disease, politics, business, labor, students, and minorities, and they have been chased out of the studios." [2]

From the consumer's vantage point, no matter how objective and fair the journalists try to be, or how often the Fairness Doctrine is applied, an *equal opportunity* to compete for public acceptance seems impossible unless each viewpoint has the same opportunity to produce its own news and entertainment and to make the big media decisions on its own. Is it possible for your opposition to represent your ideas to the public in an unbiased or fair manner? Can you expect a media executive to make a big decision that will result in his viewpoint's being discredited or in his losing a large sum of money? That is like expecting a quarterback in the super bowl to judge whether there has been pass interference on a play that determines the championship and an extra $10,000 for each player. As Frank Shakespeare, former head of the United States Information Agency, put it:

> Can 10 liberals in a room over an extended period of time, by trying hard, be fair to the conservative position: In my judgment, no—any more than 10 conservatives over an extended period of time can be fair to the liberal position. In my view, fairness comes in the mix, in the clash of ideas in the marketplace. That's where the real fairness is, in the give-and-take of ideas. [3]

Like Shakespeare, those who see bias, propaganda, and censorship as inseparable elements of any information product do not expect their opposition or themselves to be fair to each other no matter how hard they try. Furthermore, when one considers that in advertising and entertainment there is seldom, if ever, the attempt to be fair, it is hard to believe the journalists' claim that their ideas of fairness provide an equal opportunity.

If the media owners and the government cannot bring about the equal opportunities that will insure fairness, who can? The ideal solution seems obvious: we must create a situation whereby each representative viewpoint on the political spectrum is guaranteed the same amount of money, technology, and control over access to the media. This is fair to each viewpoint and, more important, will produce a marketplace of news and entertainment products that compete with equal artistic force. The "marketplace of ideas" is a concept that emphasizes the people's right to choose from among different communications products, just as they have a right to choose from among different kinds of apples, breads, or transistor radios. This competition will have the beneficial side effects of bringing about a tolerance toward other viewpoints, a flowering of artistic and journalistic talent, an increase in mental participation by the public, and a decrease in the use of the shoddier propaganda techniques. Instead of increasing polarization, this competition would tend to bring Americans closer, as all viewpoints—even those considered extreme—would be motivated to aim their messages not just to an elite few who already agree, but to the entire public in an effort toward gaining acceptance by the majority.

If a true marketplace of ideas is so desirable and beneficial, why don't we have it? There is no simple conspiracy to prevent it. Rather, it is prohibited by many factors. It takes money to buy access to or control of a newspaper or radio or television station. Without this control, a person or group is not in a position to make the important media decisions that would enable them to produce equally forceful messages. Because the poor, the radicals, and the minorities do not and will not have enough money to buy access or control of many mass media agencies, they compete at a marked disadvantage: their viewpoints are edited by the moderates and conservatives who have enough wealth to own the media and whose backgrounds, education, and experiences are such that they, or the editors they hire, will be unlikely to make decisions that will be fair to viewpoints hostile to their values or threaten their wealth. For that matter, neither are the poor likely to present fairly the viewpoints of the wealthy—assuming they were ever in a position to do so. A person's self-image, self-interests, and values are very important; it is only human nature to use the power of communication to protect or to advance one's own values and those interests favorable to oneself. Such decisions as whom to hire, where to allocate money, and what type of news, entertainment, and advertising policies to follow will, in the long run, favor the owner's viewpoints.

Media owners stand to lose money when viewpoints or proposals they dislike gain public acceptance. This of course creates conflicts of interest; media owners are not about to give equal treatment to threatening viewpoints. The conflicts of interest for media owners exist in three areas.

The first concerns the communications system itself. Broadcasting stations and newspapers are very profitable businesses. Any laws or regulations aimed at changing present practices regarding postal subsidies, cable television, advertising, license renewal, cross-media ownership, antitrust regulation, the Fairness Doctrine, or the Equal Time Provision can mean not only a loss of money, but the loss of a business. Imagine the loss of income to media agencies if no political advertising were allowed, or if broadcasters were required to give numerous hours of free time to political candidates. Imagine the loss of advertising if the American people, through their government, saw fit to establish a noncommercial public broadcast system that was given the money and technology to attract 50 percent or more of the audience. Left with a smaller audience, commercial broadcasters could not charge advertisers nearly as much money. Many democratic countries in Europe have communications systems with the features mentioned above. It is easy then to see the conflict that a media owner faces when he is confronted with the task of presenting the viewpoints of those who want to convince us that we should change our communications system.

The second conflict for some mass media owners concerns the possibility of the loss of vast sums of money if the people demand a change in some of our domestic or foreign policies. Westinghouse, AVCO, General Tire and Rubber, RCA (owner of NBC), and CBS provide services or goods for the nation's defense or space programs. A cutback in defense or space spending could mean a loss of profit for these companies. The three networks, Time Incorporated, and other media giants own or have interests in commercial broadcasting companies in other countries. They naturally want the United States to have a foreign policy that protects their interests abroad. They are also inclined to disapprove of foreign governments that forbid commercial broadcasting, foreign ownership of or investment in American mass media, or the importation of American television programs such as "The FBI," "Mannix," and "Marcus Welby." Many countries in recent years have acted to restrict the importation of such programs either to protect their own country's capacity to produce programs or to protect their people from the bias that subtly favors the U.S. economic system and its policies. The stakes involved are not small; in 1971, the sale of American television programs brought $85 million to the networks.

Policies concerning pollution and labor can also affect a media agency's profit. The *New York Times* and the *Los Angeles Times* are two newspapers that own pollution-producing paper millls; many others own mills also. All media agencies are employers of labor. It is not difficult to imagine the conflicts faced by a newspaper or a broadcasting station when it comes to presenting viewpoints in favor of defense, space, pollution, labor, and foreign policies that threaten the profits of media owners.

These two conflicts, regarding communications policy on one hand and media investments in sundry and widespread economic activities on the other, are the most compelling for media owners since they deal with policies that affect long-range and overall profits. These are also policies that are not decided directly by media executives, but by the public through the Congress and the president.

The third type of conflict of interest has little to do with political ideas. It concerns the policies needed to make profits on a short-term, day-to-day, month-to-month basis. These policies are decided by media executives. For example, the executive is faced with a conflict between presenting more and better news—which will lose money—or more popular entertainment—which will earn money. He must decide whether to cover live a golf match—which will bring in large amounts of advertising money—or a Senate hearing on a controversial topic—which will bring in no advertising money. In newspapers, magazines, or broadcasting there exist, daily, many such situations where a decision maker must decide between better informing the public or earning more through increased advertising.

In short, we have a communications system that insures that only those with vast sums of money will control the media and make the big decisions. There are of course differences among the wealthy: some are very conservative and some are moderately liberal, but they all support the same basic communications and economic system that created and protects their wealth. Their communications system inevitably expresses and promotes their values with a strong but subtle hidden bias in support of the status quo. And, because all owners are subjected to the same strong pressures, they tend to make similar decisions no matter how different their political beliefs or personal biases. It is the ownership of mass media by the wealthy, plus the shared conflicts of interest, rather than a conspiracy of any kind, that explain why the important decisions usually favor viewpoints that support things as they are rather than viewpoints that support fundamental changes in society and its communications system.

Many groups and citizens from the very conservative to the very liberal agree that the present system is inadequate and should be changed, but their proposals for how to do so differ. The very conservative critics advocate getting the government out of broadcasting completely to allow the "private property system" and the "dollar vote" of the people to determine which information agencies thrive or fail. Newspapers today operate under just such a system. Very liberal critics point out that the "dollar vote" (the people's vote for a newspaper as determined by their willingness to support it by buying it) may insure a marketplace of hot dogs or transistor radios, but it does not and cannot insure a fair marketplace of ideas in the mass media any more than the popular vote can insure justice for individuals accused of crime. For what if there are not enough customers to financially support a radical, very liberal, or far-right newspaper or radio or television station? Does that mean that these ideas should die out, and that the public-at-large should not be equally exposed to these information products through the mass media? Should antiracists be denied equal control of access just because 90 percent of the people "dollar vote" for a racist media? Should anti-Communists be denied equal control of access because 90 percent "dollar vote" for agencies that advocate coexistence?

There is an additional criticism of the "dollar vote" concept because the vote isn't always the determining factor in deciding which media will survive or fail. Advertising dollars are more important in this respect, and they do not necessarily reflect the people's choice. *Look* and *Life* magazines failed partly because they couldn't attract enough advertising, yet their circulation of seven million each showed that plenty of people gave them the "dollar vote." It seems quite possible then, that the "private property system" with its "dollar vote" support might bring to broadcasting the same drawbacks it has brought to the print media.

For public television, the very conservative critics are unanimous in wanting government money spent to support local public television stations instead of a centralized network because they feel that a centralized network tends to be liberal in orientation. Their argument has much merit, for people hired by public television at the national level do tend to be liberally oriented.

The moderate liberals and moderate conservatives suggest few changes in either the commercial or public communications system. Unlike the left and the right, they feel that even within the commercial communications system as it is, a fair marketplace of ideas can be achieved. They advocate minor reforms, such as press councils, along with professional excellence in reporting and presenting the news. They are on the whole satisfied with the present government allocations that give public broadcasting at the national level more importance than local public television.

The very conservative and very liberal critics contend that the moderate proposals will not do enough to eliminate the built-in biases of the present system.

The very liberal critics contend that both the private and the public communications systems are biased to support the status quo, be it moderately conservative or moderately liberal. Their strategy for counteracting the commercial system has been twofold. First, they are trying to force management to share its decision-making power with minority groups and reporters. Recently, large owners of broadcasting stations have agreed to minority demands to share in decision making. And at one newspaper, the *Hawk-Eye* of Burlington, Iowa, the editor-publisher has offered the reporters veto power over his choice of managing editor. But there are few such agreements, and many people doubt that such concessions by owners will make a significant difference, for no matter who makes the decisions, they are subjected to the pressures inherent in a commercial media agency.

The second strategy of the very liberal and even radical groups does not look to either the commercial communications system or to the government. They have established their own alternate communications system with "underground" weeklies, radio stations, and portable video networks. This plan has worked well in providing an alternate media, but it hasn't worked to provide a marketplace of ideas for over 90 percent of the people who still depend solely on the daily newspaper, radio, and television.

To one with a consumer's viewpoint, none of these proposals, whether from the very conservative, the moderate, or the very liberal viewpoint, seem to offer a truly satisfactory alternative to the present system. The following section asks you to come up with some suggestions of your own.

Designing an Alternative Communications System

What kind of communications system could bring about the consumer's ideal of a thriving marketplace of competitive ideas in the mass media?

First, the system should operate on the premise that overall fairness cannot be achieved, nor can censorship decisions be eliminated, by any *one* person or news agency. It seems that fairness can only be achieved when all basic viewpoints have a chance to present news and entertainment of their own, with equal money, equal technology, and equal artistic force. The end product, viewed as a totality, will thus be fair and uncensored for the consumer even if individual producers are biased and resort to censorship.

A second premise might be that given a commercial communications system, some viewpoints will probably never have the necessary political power, money, or advertising support to break into the mass media. Only if the available financial and technical capacities are distributed among all representative viewpoints can we reasonably expect thriving competition and a flowering of journalistic and artistic talent.

These two premises make imperative a vast governmental role in bringing about an adequate system. But some will wonder if this is consistent with the First Amendment: "The government shall make no law abridging freedom of the press." "Abridging" is the key word here. It is certainly constitutional if federal laws *promote* instead of abridge freedom of the press. As Supreme Court justice Hugo Black stated in 1945:

> It would be strange indeed however if the grave concern for freedom of the press which prompted adoption of the First Amendment should be read as a command that the government was without power to protect that freedom. The First Amendment . . . rests on the assumption that the widest possible dissemination of information from diverse and antagonistic sources is essential to the welfare of the public, that a free press is a condition of a free society. . . . Freedom of the press from government interference does not sanction repression of that freedom by private interests.

Even more precisely, a Canadian Senate Committee on the Mass Media stated: "If government can legislate to insure a more 'diverse and antagonistic' press, it is not interfering in freedom of the press; it is moving to protect a broader, more basic freedom: the freedom of information." The people of many democratic nations are convinced that a government role in communications is not only consistent with democracy, but that it is essential for keeping at least a part of the communications system free from the corrupting and repressive influences inevitable in a system of private ownership. As noted earlier, Italy, Germany, Israel, Holland, Denmark, and Sweden are among democracies that do not permit any private ownership of broadcasting stations. Japan, England, and Canada allow limited private commercial broadcasting, but they offset this with government-supported noncommercial stations that have the money and technology to offer the people a real alternative.

The United States also has a government-supported noncommercial broadcasting system, but that system is so restricted that it fails to offer either a marketplace of ideas or an alternative to the programming of commercial broadcasting. Both conservatives and radicals complain that it is unfair to their viewpoints, and both have an easy time proving their case.

Before deciding on the best communications role for our government, it is necessary to be aware of the basic shortcomings—aside from the obvious limitations imposed by inadequate funding—that are built into our present system of government-supported noncommercial broadcasting.

First, the system is required by law to be "fair, objective, and balanced." As we have seen, it is very difficult if not impossible for a single network to achieve this.

Second, local station managers are free to reject nationally scheduled programs that they find too controversial.

The third factor restricting public broadcasting is the makeup of the board of directors at both the local and the network levels. Most board members are not journalists representing different viewpoints, but bankers, businessmen, station managers, and university presidents—those who tend to have vested interests in the status quo.

Fourth, whatever money public broadcasting receives has strings attached. Funding is on a year-to-year basis; thus, broadcast executives are responsive to both subtle and direct congressional or administration intimidation. Corporate foundation money, which accounts for about 11 percent of public broadcasting revenue, supposedly carries no strings, but can anyone expect a family or corporation foundation to support programming that attacks the interests of its founder?

Fifth, the public broadcasting system allows corporate and foundation money to affect programming by permitting sponsorship. (Credit for sponsorship is noted before and after, but not during, the program.) Certain programs are more likely to be viewed by the public simply because some foundation or corporation will pay for them; other programs are not presented or even imagined because there is no potential corporate or foundation sponsor.

THE CHALLENGE

It is now time for you to apply what you have learned about decision making, propaganda, bias, and fairness. Your task is to design a public broadcasting system that will—from your viewpoint—offer the vital and robust marketplace of ideas that a commercial system has difficulty providing.

In answering the following questions you will be constructing a communications system. Every type of public broadcasting system in any country has to deal with these fundamental questions in one way or another. Keep in mind that there are no right answers or answers that everyone will agree with. What is important is that you can defend your answers as reasonable and effective measures for creating a real marketplace of competing ideas.

1. On the public broadcasting system that you envision, will product advertising be allowed?

2. Will political advertising be allowed?

3. Will corporate sponsorship of programs be allowed?

4. Will foundation grants or sponsorship be allowed?

5. Should money for the public broadcasting system be approved every year or be granted on a long-term or permanent basis?

6. Should the public broadcasting system consist of only one national network to produce news and entertainment that represents "fairly" all viewpoints, or should it consist of four or more national networks, each designed and staffed to produce news and entertainment from different viewpoints on the political spectrum?

7. How much money should be allocated to the one network or to each of the several networks—an amount comparable to that available to commercial networks, or a smaller amount?

8. What kind of taxes should pay for this system: taxes on advertising in commercial broadcasting, taxes on the profits of commercial broadcasting, taxes on the sale of radios and television sets, taxes on legalized gambling, taxes on income, taxes on television set owners, or a combination of these?

9. What should be the personal and professional qualifications of members of the board of directors?

10. What kind of occupations should be represented on the board of directors? For instance, for a board of thirteen members, how many, if any, should be bankers, businessmen, union leaders, journalists, professors, artists, or laymen?

11. What percentage, if any, of the boards of directors should be from minority groups such as blacks and Chicanos? What percentage, if any, should be women?

12. How should the members of the boards of directors be chosen: by the president, by a congressional committee after open hearings and applications, or by public elections?

13. Should the public broadcasting system have equal, superior, or inferior radio and television technology and airwave access compared to the commercial system? This technology involves airwave frequencies, computers, transmitters, and communications satellites.

14. If you have chosen only one network to represent all viewpoints, will the Fairness Doctrine still be necessary? If you have chosen several different networks to represent their own viewpoints, will the Fairness Doctrine be necessary?

15. After your public broadcasting system is in operation, should the Fairness Doctrine still apply to commercial broadcasting? If so, should it automatically be applied to advertising having implied or direct political messages?

16. How should the system operate to make sure that each political candidate has an equal chance to reach the public?

17. Should the Equal Time Provision apply to the new public broadcasting system? (Make this answer consistent with your answer for question number 16.) Should the provision still apply to commercial broadcasting?

18. If still in use, should the Equal Time Provision be changed to prevent the wealthier candidate from buying more broadcast time than his opponents?

19. What percentage of prime time programming should be produced by the local public broadcasting stations as compared to the national network or networks? What percentage of prime time programming should be devoted to public affairs?

20. Once the percentage of national prime time programming is established, should local public broadcasting stations have the right to reject a nationally scheduled network program or documentary?

21. Should the administrative and financial structure of the new public broadcasting system be designed so that the government has no editorial control or influence over content or programming?

Did you find these decisions difficult to make? The proposals you made may not be perfect, but in all likelihood you have designed a system that is less confused, and guarantees and promotes a freer and more equal marketplace of ideas, than our present public broadcasting system. As consumers of mass media products we can demand no less than this. Our greatest challenge is to bring it about. For we as individuals and as a country cannot meet *any* challenge, no matter what our intentions, talent, wealth, or strength may be, if we make decisions based on inadequate information products.

Books for Further Study

Bagdikian, Ben. *The Information Machines: Their Impact on Men and the Media.* New York: Harper & Row, 1971. The future of communications and their possible impact on man and society.

Carnegie Commission on Educational Television. *Public Television: A Program for Action.* New York: Bantam Books, 1967.

Emery, Walter B. *National and International Systems of Broadcasting: Their History, Operation and Control.* East Lansing, Mich.: Michigan State University Press, 1969.

Shamberg, Michael. *Guerrilla Television.* New York: Holt, Rinehart, and Winston, 1971. How to establish your own television network through the use of portable video units.

Improving the Present Communications System

It may take quite a few years to convince the public of the need to establish a new broadcasting system such as the one you have just designed, but in the meantime there are many things you can do to improve the mass media.

NEWSPAPERS

Newspapers are private property and are not required by law to serve the public interest. As a result, daily newspapers don't lend themselves easily to citizen involvement. However, a citizen or a group can still do some things to improve the local daily paper. Your town may be one of the few that has set up a press council to review citizen complaints about newspaper coverage. If so, attend the meetings. If you have a complaint, make it specific and gather enough evidence to support your case effectively before the council. If there is no press council in your area, contact the journalism or English department of the local college or university to find out if any groups are trying to get one established. You may be able to help them convince the community that there is a need for a press council.

If you find a definite pattern of biased coverage of some issue, cut out all the articles on that topic and make a comparative study of how each viewpoint is getting treated. Then write up your study and try to get it published in your school paper, local underground paper, or a journalism review. Try also to arrange a meeting with an editor of the paper you have criticized, and, using your evidence, try to convince him to avoid the unfair treatment you have discovered and documented.

COMMERCIAL BROADCASTING

You own the airwaves; the broadcasters can only lease them from your government on the condition of serving the public interest. There are laws and regulations that are theoretically designed to help you make sure the local stations deserve to keep on broadcasting. Every three years a station must prove, to the FCC's satisfaction, that it has operated in the public interest. In addition to abiding by the Fairness Doctrine and Equal Time Provision, every station is supposed to ascertain community needs and interests and then to provide appropriate programming.

Working on your own or in a group, monitor and analyze the programming of local stations. If you feel a station's overall programming does not serve local needs or that it is violating the Fairness Doctrine by airing personal attacks or unbalanced news and public-affairs features, take your complaint and proof to the station management. Try also to get your information and analysis printed in a local publication. Especially if one station in an area is noticeably better than the others, the inferior stations may be shamed into offering better programming. (To obtain a concise and helpful manual on how to use the Fairness Doctrine to counter unfair broadcasts, write to the Institute for American Democracy, 1750 Pennsylvania Avenue, NW, Washington, D.C. 20006 for *How to Combat Air Pollution*, $.50.)

If the offending station does not respond to your satisfaction, then take your case to the FCC. Use your evidence in a petition to deny the renewal of that station's license. You can also participate in any peti-

tion to prevent the transfer of station ownership to
another company that you feel has not served, or
will not serve, local needs.

Before engaging in any of these activities, be sure
to read *How to Talk Back to Your Television Set* by
former FCC commissioner Nicholas Johnson. This
book explains the petition process in simple detail. It
also lists free materials you can write for, and the
names and addresses of the many groups across the
country that are organized for the purpose of improving broadcasting.

ALTERNATIVE MEDIA

There is one major limitation in working with commercial mass media: you are ultimately dependent on
the news agencies themselves to reform policies or to
improve their product. Little can be done about this
because it is so expensive to buy a station or a newspaper or to produce a documentary film that might
meet technical and journalistic standards. However,
if you are fortunate, you may live in one of the few
cities that has a noncommercial, listener-sponsored
radio station or even a listener-sponsored television
station (KVST in Los Angeles). Besides welcoming
your financial support, these stations encourage your
help in running the station or in producing programs.
Contact the station to find out how you can help.

Portable video systems allow you to produce your
own television programs at a cost any group can afford. But you shouldn't be satisfied with showing your
programs to friends or to other groups that already
think as you do. This would have only minor impact
on your community and nation. If you are interested
in providing everyone in your community with a real
alternative to the television they have been watching
for twenty years, then you will want to make sure you
can get your program shown over cable television.
The FCC has already made a ruling requiring cable

television operations to provide a public access channel for citizen use. There is probably a citizens' group
in your community that is working to make sure this
access channel becomes a practical reality. By negotiating with the cable company, your group may be
able to achieve even more channel access plus free
use of technical facilities and a small share of profits
to subsidize citizen productions. If the cable franchise
hasn't been awarded yet, you can try to convince the
city council to demand these conditions as part of the
franchise agreement. You may even want to advocate
that your city, instead of franchising a private cable
company, own the cable system. (San Bruno, California, is one of the few cities that have opted for
municipal ownership.)

Learning how to use portable video equipment and
teaching others to use it is as important as negotiating
with the cable company. It is of little value to be able
to produce a program if it doesn't get to the public,
but it is also of little value to have free channel access
if you don't know how to produce a program. Again,
the public-interest group that is concerned with cable
in your community should be helpful in setting up
training programs. Video is simple enough for even
grade school children to use, but you can make it a
powerful tool for creating real alternatives to the
commercial mass media.

Your attempt to understand and improve mass
media cannot help but produce benefits. Learning
more about your country's information system helps
you to understand society, other citizens, and yourself. At the very least, you will search out a wider
spectrum of ideas, discriminate between good and bad
information products, and detect many forms of bias
hidden in decision making. Spotting bias makes you
less vulnerable to unbalanced news and entertainment products and thus should increase your freedom
of choice.

At the very most, you may influence your congressman or senator to support a viable noncommercial

broadcast system similar to the one you designed earlier. This may take some time. In the meantime you may be able to free your cable system for citizen productions and produce a program that has a significant impact on your community, and possibly, even the nation.

Books for Further Study

Frederiksen, H. Allan. *Community Access Video*. Berkeley, Calif.: Book People, 1972. An outstanding community organizer shows how to operate a portable video unit and tells how to gain community access to cable television.

Johnson, Nicholas. *How to Talk Back to Your Television Set*. New York: Bantam Books, 1970. How to improve television—by a former commissioner of the FCC.

Keeley, Joseph. *The Left-Leaning Antenna: A Political Bias in Television*. New Rochelle, N.Y.: Arlington House, 1971. By a former editor of *American Legion* magazine. Includes a chapter on how to improve television.

Skornia, Harry J. *Television and Society: An Inquest and Agenda for Improvement*. New York: McGraw-Hill, 1965. By the former president of the National Association of Educational Broadcasters.

Sloan Commission, *On the Cable: The Television of Abundance*. New York: McGraw-Hill, 1971. Recommendations for the future development of cable.

Appendix A

MAGAZINES FOR FURTHER STUDY

AIM Report (Accuracy in Media). 425 Thirteenth Street, NW, Washington, D.C. 20004.

Broadcasting, The Businessweekly of Television and Radio. 1735 De Sales Street, NW, Washington, D.C. 20036.

Chicago Journalism Review. 192 North Clark Street, Chicago, Illinois 60601.

Columbia Journalism Review. 700 Journalism Building, Columbia University, New York, New York 10027.

Editor and Publisher. 850 Third Avenue, New York, New York 10022.

Homefront. Institute for American Democracy, 1750 Pennsylvania Avenue, NW, Washington, D.C. 20006.

Journal of Broadcasting. Association for Professional Broadcasting Education, Temple University, Philadelphia, Pennsylvania 19122.

Journalism Quarterly. Association for Education in Journalism, University of Minnesota, Minneapolis, Minnesota 55455.

Media and Consumer. Consumers Union, 256 Washington Street, Mount Vernon, New York 10550.

More: A Journalism Review. Box 2971, Grand Central Station, New York, New York 10017.

Public Opinion Quarterly. Columbia University Press, 136 South Broadway, Irvington-on-Hudson, New York 10533.

Quill. Sigma Delta Chi, Professional Journalistic Society, 35 East Wacker Drive, Chicago, Illinois 60601.

Southern California Review of Journalism. 6101 East Seventh Street, Long Beach, California 90840.

Television Quarterly, National Academy of Television Arts and Sciences, 7188 Sunset Boulevard, Hollywood, California 90046.

TV Guide. 250 King of Prussia Road, Radnor, Pennsylvania 19088.

Variety. 154 West Forty-sixth Street, New York, New York 10036.

Appendix B

Spectrum Classification of National Weekly or Monthly Publications Dealing With Public Affairs
(Circulation figures for 1972)

Usually classified as radical or very liberal		Usually classified as liberal, middle of the road, or conservative		Usually classified as very conservative or far right	
Black Panther	10,000	Atlantic	330,000	*American Legion	2,600,000
Guardian	28,000	Atlas	125,000	American Mercury	11,000
Liberation	10,000	Commentary	62,000	American Opinion	43,000
Los Angeles Free Press	90,000	Commonweal	29,000	Barron's	493,000
Militant	10,000	*Ebony	1,200,000	Battleline	54,000
Ms.	400,000	Fortune	568,000	Christian Beacon	125,000
Muhammad Speaks	400,000	Harper's	359,000	Citizen	25,000
New York Review of Books	92,000	*Issues Today	1,000,000	Crusade Weekly	133,000
People's World	10,000	Nation	29,000	Human Events	86,000
Progressive Labor	5,000	National Observer	473,000	Liberty Letter	130,000
Ramparts	125,000	New Republic	150,000	Life Lines	5,000
Village Voice	150,000	*Newsweek	2,500,000	National Review	120,000
Washington Monthly	25,000	Progressive	40,000	New Guard	13,000
Weekly People	2,000	*Reader's Digest	18,000,000	Twin Circle	85,000
		Saturday Review	620,000	*V.F.W. Magazine	1,500,000
		*Senior Scholastic	2,800,000	Wanderer	27,000
		*Time	4,200,000	Washington Report (American Security Council)	41,000

*mass circulation (over 1,000,000)

Appendix C

BOOKS FOR MORE EXTENSIVE STUDY

SEMANTICS AND REPORTING

Adler, Ruth. *A Day in the Life of The New York Times.* Philadelphia: Lippincott, 1971. The inside story of how the *Times* is put together every day.

Balk, Alfred, and Boylan, James, eds. *Our Troubled Press.* Boston: Little, Brown & Co., 1971. A collection of articles from the *Columbia Journalism Review.*

Condon, John C., Jr. *Semantics and Communication.* New York: Macmillan Co., 1966. An introductory treatment.

Fisher, Paul. *Race and the News Media.* New York: Praeger, 1967.

Lang, Kurt and Gladys. *Television and Politics.* Chicago: Quadrangle Books, 1968. Two journalists take a critical look at television's political coverage.

Leamer, Laurence. *The Paper Revolutionaries: The Rise of the Underground Press.* New York: Simon & Schuster, 1972.

Lee, Dorothy. *Freedom and Culture.* Englewood Cliffs, N.J.: Prentice-Hall, 1959. Essays on semantics from an anthropological viewpoint.

Liebling, A. J. *The Press.* New York: Ballantine Books, 1961. A critical appraisal of press performance.

MacDougall, A. Kent. *The Press: A Critical Look from the Inside.* Princeton, N.J.: Dow Jones & Co., 1972. By a former reporter for the *Wall Street Journal.*

MacDougall, Curtis D. *Interpretive Reporting.* New York: Macmillan Co., 1968. A text for college journalism students.

MacNeil, Robert. *The People Machine: The Influence of Television on American Politics.* New York: Harper & Row, 1968.

Newfield, Jack. *Bread and Roses Too.* New York: E. P. Dutton, 1971. Essays by an advocacy journalist.

Pei, Mario. *Double-Speak in America.* New York: Hawthorn, 1973.

Safire, William. *The New Language of Politics.* New York: Macmillan, 1972. A guide to the use and misuse of language by political leaders.

Talese, Gay. *The Kingdom and the Power.* New York: Bantam Books, 1970. A study of th influence of the top executives of the *New York Times* by a former *Times* reporter.

Wolfe, Tom. *The New Journalism,* New York: Harper & Row, 1973. An anthology of new journalism with an introduction by a leading advocate.

CENSORSHIP

Aronson, James. *The Press and the Cold War.* Indianapolis: Bobbs-Merrill, 1970. An examination of the degree to which the press has become a voluntary arm of the government.

Brendze, Ruth. *Not to Be Broadcast.* New York: Vanguard Press, 1973. Censorship in the early years of radio.

Ladd, Bruce. *Crisis in Credibility.* New York: New American Library, 1972. How the government manipulates and conceals information.

Lane, Mark. *A Citizen's Dissent.* Greenwich, Conn.: Fawcett World Library, 1968. An analysis of press bias and censorship in the reporting of the assassination of President John F. Kennedy.

McGaffin, William, and Knoll, Erwin. *Anything But the Truth: The Credibility Gap; How the News Is Managed in Washington.* New York: G. P. Putnam's Sons, 1968.

Minor, Dale. *The Information War.* New York: Hawthorne Books, 1970. The conflict between the media and government, with emphasis on radio.

Phelan, John, S.J., ed. *Communications Control.* New York: Sheed & Ward, 1969. Readings in the motives and structure of censorship.

Schumack, Murray. *The Face on the Cutting Room Floor.* New York: William Morrow, 1964. Censorship of television and the movies.

Seldes, George. *Never Tire of Protesting.* New York: Lyle Stuart, 1968. A summing up of a career of an outstanding critic of the press.

Skornia, Harry J. *Television and News: A Critical Appraisal.* Palo Alto, Calif.: Pacific Books, 1968. Reveals cases of censorship along with shortcomings of television news.

The Commercial and Technical Structure of Mass Media—The Effects

Baker, Robert, and Ball, Sandra, eds. *Mass Media and Violence.* Washington, D.C.: U.S. Government Printing Office, 1969. A government commission staff report on the causes of violence.

Carpenter, Edmund. *Oh, What a Blow That Phantom Gave Me!* New York: Holt, Rinehart, and Winston, 1973. An anthropologist reports on the cultural impact of electronic media.

Friendly, Fred. *Due to Circumstances Beyond Our Control.* New York: Random House, 1967. The fight for good documentary telecasting by the former head of CBS-TV News.

Hall, Stuart, and Whannel, Paddy. *The Popular Arts.* New York: Random House, 1964.

Innis, Harold. *The Bias of Communication.* Toronto: University of Toronto Press, 1964. A historical survey of bias and the technology of communications.

Kuhns, William. *Exploring Television.* Chicago: Loyola University Press, 1971. An inquiry-discover approach.

MacDougall, Curtis D. *The Press and Its Problems.* Dubuque, Iowa: William C. Brown & Co., 1964.

Mayer, Martin. *About Television.* New York: Harper & Row, 1972.

O'Hara, Robert. *Media for the Millions: The Process of Mass Communications.* New York: Random House, 1961. A penetrating analysis of bias in entertainment programs.

Rissover, Fredric, and Birch, David C. *Mass Media and the Popular Arts.* New York: McGraw-Hill, 1971.

Rivers, William. *The Opinionmakers.* Boston: Beacon Press, 1967. How government officials use reporters and how reporters use government officials.

Rucker, Bryce. *First Freedom.* Carbondale, Ill.: University of Southern Illinois Press, 1968. A classic study of the structure and performance of the press as it relates to freedom of the press.

Sandman, Peter. *Media: An Introductory Analysis of American Mass Communications.* Englewood Cliffs, N.J.: Prentice-Hall, 1972.

Sarson, Evelyn, ed. *Action for Children's Television.* New York: Avon, Discus Books, 1971. The effect on children of television programming and advertising.

Seldes, Gilbert. *The New Mass Media: Challenge to a Free Society.* Washington, D.C.: Public Affairs Press, 1968.

Whale, John. *Half Shut Eye*. London: Macmillan & Co., 1969. The bias inherent in the technology of television reporting. By a British reporter.

The Public Interest

Goulart, Ronald. *Assault on Childhood*. Los Angeles: Sherbourne Press, 1969. An analysis of advertising and its effects on children.

Peterson, Theodore, et al. *The Mass Media and Modern Society*. New York: Holt, Rinehart, and Winston, 1965. The social aspects of mass media—a college text.

Schiller, Herbert. *Mass Communications and American Empire*. Clifton, N.J.: Augustus M. Kelly, 1969. An examination of the structure of communication ownership and the extension of American broadcasting into other countries. Challenges the idea that increased communications are necessarily desirable.

Stavins, Ralph L., ed. *Television Today: The End of Communication and the Death of Community*. Washington, D.C.: Communication Service Corporation, 1969. The story of some interesting challenges to license renewals.

Advertising

Baker, Samm. *The Permissible Lie: The Inside Truth about Advertising*. Boston: Beacon Press, 1971.

Carpenter, Edmund. *They Became What They Beheld*. New York: Ballantine Books, 1970. A distinguished anthropologist explains and depicts how methods of relating to objects and information shape people.

Della Femina, Jerry. *From Those Wonderful Folks Who Brought You Pearl Harbor*. New York: Simon & Schuster, 1970. An insider's view of advertising.

Howard, John, and Hulbert, James. *Advertising and the Public Interest*. Chicago: Crain Communications, 1973. An analysis of Federal Trade Commission hearings regarding deception and manipulation in advertising.

Mayer, Martin. *Madison Avenue, U.S.A.* New York: Pocket Books, 1963. A study of advertising.

McGinnis, Joe. *The Selling of the President*. New York: Trident Press, 1968. An inside view of how Richard Nixon used television in the 1968 campaign.

Packard, Vance. *The Hidden Persuaders*. New York: Pocket Books, 1959. The psychological aspects of advertising.

Perry, James M. *The New Politics: The Expanded Technology of Political Manipulation.* London: Weidenfeld, 1968. A study of information management on political campaigns.

Sandage, Charles H. *The Promise of Advertising.* Homewood, Ill.: Richard D. Irwin, 1961.

PROPAGANDA

Boorstin, Daniel J. *The Image: A Guide to Pseudo-Events in America.* New York: Harper & Row, 1964.

Choukas, Michael. *Propaganda Comes of Age.* Washington, D.C.: Public Affairs Press, 1965.

Doig, Ivan and Carol. *News: A Consumer's Guide.* Englewood Cliffs, N.J.: Prentice-Hall, 1972.

Ellul, Jacques. *Propaganda: The Formation of Men's Attitudes.* New York: Alfred A. Knopf, 1965.

Hoover, J. Edgar. *Masters of Deceit.* New York: Holt, Rinehart, 1958. An analysis of Communist propaganda in the U.S. by the late director of the FBI.

Kominsky, Morris. *The Hoaxers.* Boston: Branden Press, 1970. A thorough examination of far-right claims and propaganda techniques.

Lee, Alfred M. *How to Understand Propaganda.* New York: Rinehart, 1952.

Lee, Alfred M. and Elizabeth. *The Fine Art of Propaganda.* New York: Octagon Books, 1971. A study of Father Coughlin's radio speeches in the 1930s.

Mitchell, Malcolm G. *Propaganda, Polls, and Public Opinion: Are the People Being Manipulated?* Englewood Cliffs, N.J.: Prentice-Hall, 1970.

Ross, Irwin. *Image Merchants.* Garden City, N.Y.: Doubleday, 1959. An analysis of public relations practices and their effect on the press.

Wells, Alan, ed. *Mass Media and Society.* Palo Alto, Calif.: National Press Books, 1972. Readings covering every aspect of propaganda in the mass media.

Notes

CHAPTER 1.

1. Erwin Knoll, "What We Now Know," *The Progressive*, August 1971, p. 16.

2. "Walter Cronkite," CBS television, 29 October 1968.

3. Robert OHara, *Media for the Millions* (New York: Random House, 1961), pp. 239–40.

4. Ruth Brendze, *Not to Be Broadcast* (New York: Vanguard Press, 1937), p. 197.

5. Brik Barnouw, quoted in "Conspiracy of Silence," Westinghouse Broadcasting Company, radio documentary, 1966.

6. *Providence Journal and Evening Bulletin*, 6–8, 13–16 October 1958, reprinted in *Readings in Public Opinion and Propaganda*, eds. Reo Christenson and Robert McWilliams (New York: McGraw-Hill, 1962), p. 149.

7. John Merrell, "How *Time* Stereotyped Three U.S. Presidents," *Journalism Quarterly*, Autumn 1965, p. 563.

8. Edith Efron, *The News Twisters* (Los Angeles: Nash Publishing Co., 1971), p. 108.

CHAPTER 2.

1. *Columbia Journalism Review*, May/June 1972, p. 4; *New York Times*, 27 January 1972, p. 36; *Variety*, 26 January 1972, p. 29.

2. *Los Angeles Times*, 2 February 1970, p. 1.

3. John Hohenberg, *The News Media* (New York: Holt, Rinehart, and Winston, 1968), p. 92; *New York Times*, 10 August 1966, p. 4.

4. *Chicago Journalism Review*, August 1971, p. 9.

5. 24 February 1968.

6. *Los Angeles Times*, 25 June 1968, p. 1.

CHAPTER 3.

1. 26 January 1970.

2. Jean Kerrick, "The Influence of Captions on Picture Inter-

pretation," *Journalism Quarterly*, Spring 1955, p. 177; Reuben Mehling, "Attitude Changing Effect of News and Photo Combinations," *Journalism Quarterly*, Spring 1959, p. 187.

3. *Chicago Journalism Review*, November 1971, p. 11.

4. Edward J. Epstein, *News from Nowhere* (New York: Random House, 1973), pp. 20–21.

5. *Washington Daily News*, 2 October 1969; *Columbia Journalism Review*, Fall 1969, p. 55.

6. Joseph Keeley, *The Left-Leaning Antenna* (New Rochelle, N.Y.: Arlington House, 1971), p. 35.

CHAPTER 4.

1. *AP Review*, September 1970, reprinted in *Columbia Journalism Review*, May/June 1971, p. 30.

2. *AIM Report*, August and December 1972; story concerning evidence, July 26; concerning dismissal, October 25.

3. *Newsweek*, 14 September 1959, p. 94; U.S. Senate, Committee on Commerce, *Freedom of Communications*, 1961, Report 994, part 4, p. 1030.

4. *More*, December 1972, p. 2; ibid., January 1973, p. 19.

5. Peter Lance, *More*, December 1971, p. 8.

6. Les Brown, *Television* (New York: Harcourt Brace Jovanovich, 1971), p. 221.

CHAPTER 5.

1. Nat Hentoff, *Village Voice*, 22 April 1971, p. 42; *New York Times*, UPI photograph, 4 April 1971, section IV, p. 4.

2. John Hohenberg, *The News Media* (New York: Holt, Rinehart, and Winston, 1968), p. 127.

3. Edward J. Epstein, *News from Nowhere* (New York: Random House, 1973), pp. 18, 23, 179, 247, 255.

4. Joseph Keeley, *The Left-Leaning Antenna* (New Rochelle, N.Y.: Arlington House, 1971), pp. 36–37.

5. Jules Witcover, "Loeb vs. Muskie," *Columbia Journalism Review*, May/June 1972, p. 16.

6. *Variety*, 7 February 1973, p. 32.

7. James Keogh, *President Nixon and the Press* (New York: Funk and Wagnalls, 1972), p. 75.

8. Robert Cirino, *Don't Blame the People* (New York: Vintage Books, 1972), p. 257.

CHAPTER 6.

1. 19 February 1972.
2. "Nixon, How the Press Suppressed the News," *New Republic*, 6 October 1952, p. 11.
3. Robert Cirino, *Don't Blame the People* (New York: Vintage Books, 1972), pp. 26–27.
4. *New York Times*, 8 April 1960, p. 16.
5. *AIM Report*, September 1972; *New York Times*, 13 August 1972; ibid., 14 August 1972.
6. *New York Times*, 4 September 1971, p. 45.
7. 4 September 1971.

CHAPTER 7.

1. *Chicago Journalism Review*, February 1972, p. 8.
2. Lester Markel, as quoted by William Rivers in "The New Confusion," *The Progressive*, December 1971, p. 26.
3. Albert Mehrabian, *Tactics of Social Influence* (Englewood Cliffs, N.J.: Prentice-Hall, 1970), p. 94.
4. Joyce Brothers, "The President and the Press," *TV Guide*, 23 September 1972, p. 7.
5. *Los Angeles Times*, 5 May 1972, p. 30.
6. Edith Efron, *The News Twisters* (Los Angeles: Nash Publishing Co., 1971), pp. 32–46.
7. "Huntley-Brinkley," NBC television, 3 November 1969.
8. "Walter Cronkite," CBS television, 5 September 1969.
9. "Douglas Edwards," CBS television, 11 August 1972.
10. James Keogh, *President Nixon and the Press* (New York: Funk and Wagnalls, 1972), p. 80.
11. 16 July 1969.
12. *Los Angeles Times*, 5 May 1972, p. 30.

CHAPTER 8.

1. Robert Cirino, *Don't Blame the People* (New York: Vintage Books, 1972), pp. 280–81.
2. *New York Times*, 7 April 1961; p. 2; William McGaffin and Irwin Knoll, *Anything But the Truth* (New York: G. P. Putnam's Sons, 1961), p. 179.
3. "CBS Special on the Pentagon Papers," July 1971.
4. *Ramparts*, Newsletter, 5 September 1972.
5. "CIA Recruiting" *Parade*, 12 November 1972; James Otis, "Spooks on Parade," *Ramparts*, March 1973, p. 20.

6. *Columbia Journalism Review,* special issue on the Pentagon Papers, September/October 1971.

CHAPTER 9.

1. Dwight Whitney, "I Want it on the Air," *TV Guide,* 4 July 1970, p. 5.

2. Robert Cirino, *Don't Blame the People* (New York: Vintage Books, 1972), p. 87.

3. Erik Barnouw, *The Image Empire* (New York: Oxford University Press, 1970), p. 158.

4. Ibid.

5. Howard Felsher, "The President Was Willing," *TV Guide,* 24 October 1970, p. 6.

6. Ibid., p. 10.

7. *New York Times,* 17 October 1971, section II, p. 19; ibid., 6 October 1971, p. 94; ibid., 7 October 1971, p. 93.

8. Robert Shayon, *Saturday Review,* 4 December 1971, p. 68.

9. Maury Green, *Los Angeles Times,* 18 December 1972, section IV.

10. "Washington Post Service" in *Honolulu Advertiser,* 11 January 1973, p. A5; Elmer Lower on "The Advocates," PBS, 4 March 1973.

11. Steve Knof, *Variety,* 3 September 1969, p. 33.

CHAPTER 10.

1. *Survey of Broadcast Journalism: 1970–71* (New York: Grosset & Dunlap), p. 32.

2. "Local Blackouts on Public Affairs Television," *Columbia Journalism Review,* Spring 1962, p. 40; "Local Blackouts of Network Television: A Second Look," ibid., Spring 1966, p. 22.

3. *Variety,* 13 June 1973, p. 29.

4. Edward J. Epstein, *News from Nowhere* (New York: Random House, 1973), p. 55.

5. Les Brown, *Television* (New York: Harcourt Brace Jovanovich, 1971), p. 360.

6. *Survey of Broadcast Journalism: 1968–69* (New York: Grosset & Dunlap), p. 15.

7. *Variety,* 27 September 1961, pp. 25, 46; *New York Times,* 20 September 1961, p. 59.

8. *Survey of Broadcast Journalism: 1968–69,* p. 15.

9. Brown, *Television,* p. 328.

10. *Columbia Journalism Review,* Spring 1970, p. 6.

11. *New York Times,* 11 October 1972, p. 87.

CHAPTER 11.

1. Drew Pearson, *The Case Against Congress* (New York: Simon & Schuster, 1968), pp. 429–31.

2. *The Journalists Newsletter*, Providence, R.I., March 1973, pp. 1–4.

3. Correspondence with the author; Edward Sorel, *Making the World Safe for Hypocrisy* (Chicago: Swallow Press, 1972). Mark McIntire, "Muting Megaphone Mark," *More*, July 1973, p. 5.

4. *Columbia Journalism Review*, July/August 1971, p. 5.

5. *Columbia Journalism Review*, September 1972, p. 6; January 1973, p. 8.

6. *Chicago Journalism Review*, March 1973, p. 3.

CHAPTER 12.

1. *New York Times*, 7 March 1973, p. 87; *Honolulu Advertiser*, 7 March 1973, p. 1.

2. *Honolulu Star-Bulletin*, 7 July 1971, p. 2.

3. *Los Angeles Times*, 17 February 1969, section IV, p. 26; UPI story in *Stars and Stripes*, Fulda, West Germany, 12 June 1969; Nat Hentoff, "Smothers Brothers: Who Controls TV?", *Look*, 24 June 1969, p. 27.

4. *Honolulu Star-Bulletin*, 14 September 1967, p. 10; *New York Times*, 13 September 1967, p. 95 .

5. Paul Robeson, *Here I Stand* (Boston: Beacon Press, 1971).

6. "The Doan Report," *TV Guide*, 9 December 1972, p. A1.

7. *Variety*, 28 October 1964, p. 1; *New York Times*, 29 October 1964, p. 71.

CHAPTER 13.

1. *Honolulu Star-Bulletin*, 31 July 1972, p. B8.

2. Peter Sandman, "Who Should Police Environmental Advertising?" *Columbia Journalism Review*, January 1972, p. 44.

3. *Columbia Journalism Review*, November/December 1971, p. 4.

4. *Honolulu Star-Bulletin*, 3 August 1972, p. 20.

5. *AIM Report*, September 1972, p. 7; *Washington Star-News*, 24 August 1972.

6. Sandman, "Who Should Police Environmental Advertising?" p. 46.

7. Ibid., p. 44.

CHAPTER 14.

1. *New York Times*, 16 November 1972, p. 14.
2. Robert Cirino, *Don't Blame the People* (New York: Vintage Books, 1972), p. 90.
3. *Columbia Journalism Review*, July/August 1971, p. 6.
4. *Variety*, 21 June 1972, p. 38.
5. Robert Cassidy, *More*, April 1972, p. 3.
6. *Los Angeles Times*, 22 April 1972, p. 25.

PART III.

1. Richard Doan, "Public TV: Is Anybody Watching?", *TV Guide*, 21 August 1971, p. 5.
2. *New York Times*, 26 September 1961, p. 78.
3. Ibid., 18 September 1961, p. 83.

CHAPTER 15.

1. *Survey of Broadcast Journalism: 1970–71* (New York: Grosset & Dunlap), p. 13; *Newsweek*, 16 April 1973, p. 97.
2. Les Brown, *Television* (New York: Harcourt Brace Jovanovich, 1971), p. 16.
3. Ibid., p. 126.
4. Ibid., pp. 55, 108.
5. Ibid., p. 61.
6. *Variety*, 10 January 1973.
7. Brown, *Television*, p. 64.

CHAPTER 16.

1. Robert Cirino, *Don't Blame the People* (New York: Vintage Books, 1972), pp. 12, 34, 36, 38.
2. Ibid., p. 169.
3. Ben Bagdikian, "The Fruits of Agnewism," *Columbia Journalism Review*, January 1973, p. 12.
4. Frank Barnako, "Sound and Banter Signifying Little," *Chicago Journalism Review*, January 1972, p. 4.
5. Richard Townly, "Through the Tube Darkly," *TV Guide*, 29 May 1971, p. 44.
6. *Philadelphia Journalism Review*, August 1971, p. 10.
7. Cirino, p. 239.

CHAPTER 17.

1. Les Brown, *Television* (New York: Harcourt Brace Jovanovich, 1971), p. 221.

2. Bill Greeley, *Variety,* 28 June 1972, p. 1.

3. "Local Blackouts of Network Television," *Columbia Journalism Review,* Spring 1966, p. 22; Fred Friendly, *Due to Circumstances Beyond Our Control* (New York: Random House, 1967), pp. 212–65.

4. *Newsweek,* 6 March 1972, p. 72.

5. *Variety,* 23 May 1973, p. 43.

6. Edward J. Epstein, *News from Nowhere* (New York: Random House, 1973), p. 76.

CHAPTER 18.

1. *New York Times,* 8 March 1972, p. 67.

2. Canada, Report of the Special Senate Committee on Mass Media, *Mass Media,* Volume III (Ottawa: Queens Printer Canada, 1970), p. 200.

3. *Survey of Broadcast Journalism: 1970–71* (New York: Grosset & Dunlap), p. 12; Les Brown, *Television* (New York: Harcourt Brace Jovanovich, 1971), p. 203.

4. "Reporter as Scapegoat," *The Review of Southern California Journalism,* August 1972, p. 5.

5. *Chicago Journalism Review,* April 1970, p. 15; *Columbia Journalism Review,* Fall 1969, p. 3.

6. A. Q. Mowbray, "Free Press in Fancy Packages," *Nation,* 11 December 1967, pp. 621–23.

7. Harry Skornia, *Television and the News* (Palo Alto: Pacific Books, 1968), p. 82.

CHAPTER 19.

1. *Los Angeles Times,* 16 November 1971, p. 2; Robert Shayon, *Saturday Review,* 25 December 1971, p. 13.

2. *New York Times,* 14 November 1969, p. 24.

3. *Variety,* 11 October 1972, p. 33.

4. "Who Gets Tube Time?", *New Republic,* 19 February 1972, p. 7.

5. *Variety,* 3 May 1972, p. 1.

6. *Variety,* 11 April 1973, p. 39.

CHAPTER 20.

1. *Los Angeles Times*, 15 November 1972, p. 21.

2. *New York Times*, 17 August 1971, p. 1.

3. *Variety*, 7 February 1973, p. 32.

4. Joan Nicholson, "Now Says TV Commercials Insult Women," *New York Times Magazine*, 28 May 1972, p. 12; Lucy Komisar, "Turning Off the Tube," *Ms.*, August 1972, p. 5.

5. Robert Cassidy, "Stripping Out the Facts," *More*, April 1972, p. 4.

6. Thomas Asher, "Smoking Out Smokey the Bear," *More*, March 1972, p. 10; Julie Morris, "Auto Ads Billed as Public Service" *Chicago Journalism Review*, May 1970, p. 10.

CHAPTER 21.

1. *Los Angeles Times*, 4 June 1972, p. B.

2. *Variety*, 6 September 1972, p. 31; ibid., 18 October 1972, p. 28.

3. *Los Angeles Herald-Examiner*, 15 October 1972, p. 2.

4. Richard Doan, *TV Guide*, 26 February 1972, p. A1. *Variety*, 8 March 1972, p. 32.

5. *TV Guide*, 6 May 1972, p. 4.

6. Ibid., 26 February 1972, p. 6.

7. KNX radio newscast, Los Angeles, 11 October 1972.

8. Les Brown, *Variety*, 25 October 1972, p. 1; Bill Greeley, *Variety*, November 1972, pp. 31, 46.

9. *Variety*, 21 October 1964, p. 33.

CHAPTER 22.

1. *More*, January 1972, p. 16.

2. "What Happens to the News," Winter Soldier Investigation, Detroit, 31 January 1971, broadcast by KPFK Los Angeles radio station.

3. *New York Times*, 20 May 1972, p. 8.

4. Joseph Volzs, *New York Times*, 20 May 1972, p. 4.

5. Richard Townly, "Television Journalism," *TV Guide*, 15 May 1971, p. 10; ibid., 29 May 1971, p. 40.

6. Fred Powledge, *The Engineering of Restraint* (Washington, D.C.: Public Affairs Press, 1971), p. 18.

7. J. William Fulbright, *The Pentagon Propaganda Machine* (New York: Vintage Books, 1971), pp. 70, 72, 106.

8. *Los Angeles Times*, 20 December 1971, p. 13; Erwin

Knoll, "Background Noise," *The Progressive,* February 1972, p. 27; Ralph Nader, *Los Angeles Times,* 16 December 1972, p. 23.

9. *Columbia Journalism Review,* December 1971, p. 2.

CHAPTER 23.

1. *Los Angeles Times,* 7 February 1972, section IV, p. 18.

2. *Columbia Journalism Review,* July/August 1972, p. 5.

3. *Variety,* 22 November 1972, p. 51; January 1973, p. 35.

4. Nicholas Von Hoffman, *Honolulu Star-Bulletin,* 2 April 1972, p. 17.

5. *New York Times,* 11 May 1972, p. 91.

6. Ibid., 19 May 1972, p. 75.

7. *Newsweek,* 12 February 1973, p. 46.

8. Edward J. Epstein, *News from Nowhere* (New York: Random House, 1973), pp. 209–15.

9. Ben Bagdikian, "How Newspapers Use Columnists," *Columbia Journalism Review,* Fall 1964, p. 20.

CHAPTER 24.

1. *Columbia Journalism Review,* May/June 1972, p. 5; *Chicago Journalism Review,* February 1972, p. 10.

2. *New York Times,* 24 March 1947, p. 19; Bruce Oliver, "Thought Control—American Style," *New Republic,* 13 January 1947, p. 12. Dozier Cade, "Witch Hunting, 1952," *Journalism Quarterly,* Fall 1952, p. 404.

3. Joseph Keeley, *The Left-Leaning Antenna* (New Rochelle, N.Y.: Arlington House, 1971), p. 50.

4. Alfred Balk, "Beyond Agnewism," *Columbia Journalism Review,* Winter 1969–70, p. 16.

5. *Variety,* 14 January 1970, p. 47.

6. Balk, "Beyond Agnewism," p. 16.

CHAPTER 25.

1. *Editor and Publisher,* October and November of every presidential election year.

2. Ben Bagdikian, "The Fruits of Agnewism," *Columbia Journalism Review,* January 1973, pp. 9–24.

3. Arthur Rowse, *Slanted News* (Boston: Beacon Press, 1957).

4. Lionel Lokos, *Hysteria 1964* (New Rochelle, N.Y.: Arlington House, 1967), p. 16.

5. Ben Bagdikian, "Behold the Grassroots Press, Alas!" *Harper's,* December 1964, p. 102.

6. *Boston Globe,* 19 February 1968, p. 2A.

CHAPTER 26.

1. Robert Cirino, *Don't Blame the People* (New York: Vintage Books, 1972), pp. 223–27.

2. Ibid., pp. 285–87.

3. Joseph Keeley, *The Left-Leaning Antenna* (New Rochelle, N.Y.: Arlington House, 1971), pp. 32, 38.

4. *AIM Report,* January 1973, p. 7.

5. July 1971.

6. *Institute of American Democracy Newsletter,* June 1972, p. 44; *Chicago Sun-Time Service in Honolulu Star-Bulletin,* 29 January 1972, p. 7.

A CONSUMER'S VIEWPOINT.

1. *New York Times,* 2 June 1969, p. 14.

2. *Los Angeles Times,* 9 February, 1972, p. 5.

3. Quoted in Joseph Keeley, *The Left-Leaning Antenna* (New Rochelle, N.Y.: Arlington House, 1971), p. 51.

Index to the Cases